CW01502246

MULL

A Traveller's Guide

Companion volume
SKYE – A Traveller's Guide

MULL

A Traveller's Guide

Christine Wiener

S. Forsyth, London

© 1991 C. WIENER

Illustrations and Maps by Sophie Mason
Photographs by author
Designed and typeset by Fakenham Photosetting
Ltd, Fakenham, Norfolk
Printed by Flaircard Ltd, t/a Colourprint,
Fakenham, Norfolk
Bound by Biddles Ltd, Guildford and Kings Lynn

Published by Stuart Forsyth, 27 Longton Avenue,
London SE26 6RE

ISBN 0 9515476 1 5

Table of Contents

Tobermory

Iona Abbey

Tor Abb

I

Approaches to Mull

When David Balfour landed on Mull – on Earraid, to be precise, at the far end of the Ross of Mull – his first impressions were unfavourable. The circumstances of his arrival were not propitious: shipwrecked from the brig, piously named the *Covenant*, which was carrying him into slavery in the Carolinas, the hero of 'Kidnapped', clinging to a broken spar, landed on the little island shortly after midnight. The gale abated, but by dawn it came on to rain, and from the top of the hill David climbed in an attempt to keep warm, there was nothing to be seen but 'a jumble of granite rocks with heather in among'. There was never a habitation nor a man to be seen, and on the ocean, not a sail. David spent some time on Earraid, feeding himself on raw shell-fish, including limpets and 'buckies' before discovering that Earraid is not really an island – at low tide, the creek which divides it from the mainland is easy to ford. So David waded across to continue his adventures on Mull.

Through his fictional hero, Robert Louis Stevenson presented one aspect – the worst – of Mull. He knew his territory well: as a student in the 1870s, he had spent three weeks on Earraid itself where his father had built the lighthouse out on Dhu Heartach and a neat row of cottages on the islet to accommodate

relief helpers. Robert Louis had enjoyed his holiday immensely, as he wrote to his mother in Edinburgh, and no doubt the storm in 'Kidnapped' and the ensuing gloom were necessary to his narrative. But the bleak face Mull can show is, unfortunately, not unknown to its visitors. One of its most famous, Dr Johnson, described it as 'a most dolorous country'. This may not have been a considered judgment for Boswell tells us that Johnson was 'not in very good humour' after a hard day's riding on one of the small local horses which was all the island could provide to transport the great man's mighty bulk.

Johnson and Boswell came to Mull towards the end of their Scottish tour, sailing in to Tobermory 'safely and agreeably' on Thursday the 14th of October 1773 from the island of Coll where they had been staying with its young laird. Both men praised the harbour: 'An excellent harbour', Boswell wrote, though he noted, as Johnson did, that it was not fully protected from the prevailing winds. 'An island lies before it, and it is surrounded by a hilly theatre. The island is too low, otherwise this would be quite a secure port; but the island not being a sufficient protection, some storms blow very hard here. Not long ago, fifteen vessels were blown from their moorings.' Dr Johnson says much the same of the little port, which he calls Tobor Morar: '(It) appears to an unexperienced eye formed for the security of ships; for its mouth is closed by a small island, which admits them through narrow channels into a bason sufficiently capacious. They are indeed safe from the sea, but there is a hollow between the mountains, through which the wind issues from the land with very mischievous violence.'

There was no damage, however, on the day of his arrival and, with several other vessels anchored in the bay, Dr Johnson remarked that Tobermory had 'a very commercial appearance'. The safety or otherwise of the Hebridean ports had already been a matter of concern to earlier travellers who believed that a more prosperous future for the islands depended on developing the fishing trade. One of the first, Martin Martin, who was born in Skye and knew the Hebridean waters well, explored them again late in the seventeenth century to study their potential. Science and superstition rub shoulders in his 'Description of the Western Isles', which was dedicated to Prince George of Denmark, Queen Anne's husband, but it contains a vivid and valuable record of the Hebridean way of life. Martin was followed to Mull by another Scotsman, John Knox, who had made his fortune in England. After he retired he returned to Scotland on behalf of the newly founded British Society for Extending the Fisheries to sail the West Coast and the outlying islands.

At either end of the eighteenth century, both Martin and Knox could be said to have recorded their travels in a professional capacity. Thomas Pennant, a wealthy landowner from Wales who dedicated himself to the study of zoology, explored the Highlands and Islands in pursuit of his hobby. He arrived on Mull in 1772, a year before Johnson and Boswell, and like them, published a book based on the journal he kept during his voyage. With his scientific interests – he was a member of the Royal Society – Pennant can be said to have bridged the gap before the tourists proper came. Until his day, travelling for pleasure was virtually unheard of. Apart from the very high cost and the time involved, the eighteenth century had no taste for scenery: nature untrammelled was generally voted 'horrid'. The military were often on the move, businessmen went where trade called them, the occasional scientist or man of letters would make a journey in pursuit of his

4

researches. But the average citizen left his fireside only for family occasions, or social ones such as taking the waters at some fashionable spa, like Bath. In England, a long series of Turnpike Acts had brought some improvement to the roads along which the heavy stage coaches now rumbled; in Scotland, the highways built by General Wade to facilitate the movement of troops in pursuit of Jacobites and their Highland allies had been allowed to fall into disrepair once the action was over. Pennant himself warned of the risks attendant on travelling in those parts: 'hardihood' he said was needed 'to venture on a journey to the remotest part of North Britain'.

Real discomfort and danger not altogether imaginary were forgotten with the publication, in 1810, of Walter Scott's 'The Lady of the Lake'. Set in and around Loch Katrine, it beat all the records of poetry sales and turned the hitherto undiscovered Trossachs into a veritable tourists' Mecca. Hoping to repeat his success, Walter Scott then undertook a trip to the Inner Hebrides, during which he visited Staffa, Iona and Mull in search of local colour for another epic. 'The Lord of the Isles' was no best-seller – the public, the author and the publisher agreed that it was a 'disappointment'. But the Romantic mood had been set and the floodgates stood open.

Walter Scott had an unusual predecessor in Mrs Sarah Murray. A well-to-do widow in her early sixties, she was the author of two popular books written between 1795 and 1804 on the 'Beauties of Scotland'. Based on the journals she kept during her travels, they combined a passion for the picturesque with very practical advice. Mrs Murray was before her time in her enthusiasm for nature in the raw – storms at sea, wild mountain scenery, bare and barren moor, chasms and cascades, she pursued them all avidly. But she was perfectly level-headed when she came to describe the conditions she had to deal with – much the same as Johnson and Boswell had endured with far less good humour. Mrs Murray crossed to Mull from the isle of Rum and made for Loch na Keal, riding side saddle as ladies did, across the trackless moor. When the going got too rough, she went on foot. She forded burns and, before the days of ferries, crossed rivers in open boats. She experienced days of soaking rain and going from island to island, remained undaunted by heavy seas. This is how she described the journey from Bunessan on the Ross of Mull to the island of Eigg, a journey so rough that they were blown off course and had to seek shelter on Coll: 'We passed point after point, but no harbour appeared ... the wind was high and we steered into the Loch (Breacha-chadh) full sail. The wind was directly for us, but the tide contrary, which made the sea run high, and roar amongst the rocks. The sea was dashing, the sails rattling, the sailors hallowing and shouting.' All ended well, for after scrambling ashore, she was sheltered 'with all imaginable attention and hospitality by Colonel M'Lean and his amiable daughter and family'. (Mrs Murray's books are now hard to come by, but a vivid account of her Odyssey is given in 'The Discovery of the Hebrides' by Elizabeth Bray.)

Another, later, visitor to Mull, the poet John Keats, was in complete physical contrast to the portly widow, though he shared her Romantic tastes and stout heart. Times were changing and travel becoming less arduous, but Keats had no money. So in 1818, barely three years before his death from consumption he walked thirty-seven miles across Mull to visit Iona and Staffa. As it was, he had already covered fifteen miles on foot to reach Oban where his plans to explore the islands across the Sound were nearly defeated by the high cost of the journey by ferry. By the time Keats and his friend Charles Brown arrived, the Highlands and the Hebrides were all the rage and the boatmen's prices had risen accordingly. The two young men were about to give up Mull and make north for Fort William when a guide was found who offered to take them across country, thus saving them the expensive sea-excursion round the north of Mull. The sight of Staffa's strange rocky formation which gives it the appearance of a giant organ inspired Keats to write a poem, but Staffa is better known still through Mendelssohn's famous overture, 'The Hebrides'. The work was composed in 1829 when Felix Mendelssohn was no more than twenty and it has been described as landscape set to music. This opinion is given some substance by the young musician's reaction to his sisters' questions about the Hebrides. 'It cannot be told', he said, 'only played.'

But it can also be painted: the beautiful scenery of Mull and its many outlying islands has been recorded by a long line of artists. The aquarellist, William Daniell, spent three years, from 1818, to 1821 on his 'Voyage round the Coast of Great Britain' during which he produced many fine water-colours of beauty spots in the Western Isles. Mull is represented, among others, by an aquatint of Ben More, flanked by its attendant peaks, dominating the moorland; the view is taken from Ulva House across the Sound of that name. Some years later, William Turner travelled in these parts and left us a splendid impressionistic sea-scape of the waters round

Loch Scridain

Staffa. But it is from Daniell and his predecessors among the etchers and engravers
who accompanied expeditions to chart the
islands that modern tourists will see what the
landscape looked like then and be startled
perhaps to realise how little it has changed.

They are still there – the high mountains
with snow streaking their sides and cloud
caught in the deep gullies; the long stretches
of bare moorland, with the heather and the
bracken and the golden whin-bushes. Wide
rainbows stretch across the horizon dismiss-
ing the rain, then the sun catches the waters of
Loch na Keal which scissors the island nearly
in half, and Loch Scridain, running along the
north coast of the Ross of Mull, changes with
the wind, from sullen grey to the brightest

blue. The forest of Salen by the edge of the freshwater Loch Frisa remains to remind us that Mull was once called the 'isle of trees'. The deeply indented coast hides small coves and beaches of fine sand beneath great cliffs of basalt or granite and, to the west, a multitude of tiny islands play hide and seek as the mist rises and falls.

This is very much the landscape found in the sketches another artist, an amateur this time, provided to illustrate the journal he left of a tour of the Highlands and Islands made in the 1820s. John Eddowes Bowman, a self-made banker from the Welsh Marches, spent several weeks in the summer of 1825 travelling with his friend, John Freeman Milward Dovaston, a barrister based in nearby Shropshire. Both were men of parts who shared many interests, including natural history; they were also keen readers of Walter Scott.

They set off for Scotland on the 15th July 1825, travelling by way of Chester, Liverpool and Carlisle, where they took the coach for Glasgow. As Dovaston put it, in a jolly bit of doggerel:

'The Banker and the Barrister together
  they did ride,
To gaze on bonny Scotland's rocks and
  lakes from side to side.'

This newly discovered interest in the scenery, the wilder the better, reflects the travellers' liking for the Waverley novels, and so indeed do the opening paragraphs of Bowman's journal: 'I had for many years felt a strong desire to visit Scotland – its wild and romantic scenery; its many monuments of rude and barbarous ages; the marvellous events of its ancient and modern history; and the spirit of liberty which still lingers among its mountains, and breathes in its native poetry, had long operated as so many talismans, to allure me to its soil.'

It was just over fifty years since Dr Johnson had at last fulfilled his expressed desire to visit the Highlands, but though the mood of the times had grown romantic, conditions had changed hardly at all. The Industrial Revolution was beginning in England, but the railway age was still to come. Travelling was mainly by coach, with fast 'fliers' now available between the bigger towns. The Borders and the Lowlands had drawn nearer to England; the Highlands remained remote. However, access to the Western Islands had become easier with the establishment of a steamship service. Thus, on Tuesday July the 26th, we find Bowman and Dovaston, who had spent the night in Glasgow, hurrying down to the Broomielaw to board the Highlander steam packet which was to carry them through the Hebrides. They got on deck 'just as the Bagpipes gave the signal to get under weigh'. Down the Clyde to Rothesay, they rounded the isle of Bute, made south for Arran, then north into 'the noble Loch Fyne', touching at Tarbert and Lochgilphead. After spending a night on shore, the next day they boarded the packet which was lying at the eastern entrance of the Crinan Canal. The canal, with its fifteen locks, was cut in 1801 to save the long and dangerous journey round the rocky coast of the Mull of Kintyre. It was begun in 1793 to the plans of John Rennie and work continued after its official opening directed by Thomas Telford. They passed by Jura, then Scarba with its famous Corryvreckan whirlpool, saw Colonsay in the distance, negotiated the Sound of Luing and its archipelago, and entered the Firth of Lorn. Passing the 'interesting and beautiful' island of Kerrera they reached Oban at 'about 1 o'clock'. The journey from Glasgow had taken rather more than twenty-four hours.

Bowman recorded his first impressions of Oban: 'a small, though lively little town, which stretches along the shore of its deep and sheltered bay. The hills which rise from the shore surround it like an amphitheatre.' The fares that Bowman and Dovaston had paid at Glasgow included their passage around Mull, where they stayed at Tobermory before taking ship again to explore Staffa and Iona. Then it was back to Oban again where the packet put them ashore on its return journey to Glasgow. They intended to pursue their travels north to Fort William, but in the meantime Bowman added to his notes on Oban. 'The pretty little town owes its existence to its advantageous situation and to the fine bay on whose shore it is built. This bay is of a semi-circular form; and has two openings; one to the north and another to the south. It is sufficiently extensive to afford anchorage for five-hundred sail of vessels,

and is well defended from the western winds
. . . it seems formed by nature and a combi-
nation of many important advantages, to
become the principal place of trade for the
Highlands and the middle district of the
Western Isles.' A statement which suggests
that beneath the Romantic in pursuit of 'Caledonia, stern and wild' there lay a practical
eighteenth-century businessman. However,
Oban has also been valued for its looks. The
writer, Seton Gordon, intimately acquainted
with the Highlands, says that he knows of 'no
town in Britain with the charm of Oban'; the
Green Michelin Guide awards its surroundings two of its precious stars.

For centuries, Oban was presumably no
more than a secluded village, but its excep-
tional situation – on a wide and deep bay
practically closed off by the island of Kerrera
from the rigours of heavy seas and Atlantic
storms – did not go unnoticed by the earliest
natives. The name itself – a Gaelic one –
means 'little bay', and there is some evidence
that it may have been used by the Vikings on
their summer raids. And once the search was
on for safe anchorage for the herring fleets the
British Fisheries Society was hoping to build
up, Oban, along with Tobermory on Mull,
became one of a number of 'fishing stations',
as they were designated. The Society's emiss-
ary, John Knox, who sailed the Hebridean
waters in the 1780s, was among those to
recommend it. For a number of reasons,
among them the exorbitant tax on the salt
needed to preserve the catch, the fishing

industry in the islands and on the West Coast did not develop as much as had been hoped. The still unexplained migratory habits of the herring, the local catch with the biggest potential, were against it: huge shoals of herring would come into a loch for several years running, then move on to another or take to deeper waters out at sea.

But the way ahead lay open for Oban: if it failed partly as a commercial port, it soon succeeded as a tourist resort. According to a Victorian guide book, which calls Oban 'a handsome town', it had become 'the most fashionable of Scottish watering-places' by 1791, and with the establishment of a regular steamship service from Glasgow, its prosperity grew apace. In 1773, Dr Johnson dismissed Oban with the laconic comment that it had 'a tolerable inn'; nowadays, an uninterrupted row of hotels stretch along the Craggan, as the esplanade is called, with fine views over the Sound of Mull. A twenty-minute walk brings one to the ivy-covered ruins of Dunolly Castle, the ancestral seat of one of the district's leading families. The MacDougalls are descended from Somerled, the twelfth century Lord of the Isles; they take their name, which means 'black stranger', from his eldest son, Dougall. Through him they held the title of Lords of Lorne for a time. But lands and title passed to the Stewarts in 1388 when the MacDougall clan chief died without male issue. The eldest daughter of the MacDougall chief, however, still holds the courtesy title of 'Maid of Lorne'. It was the Stewarts who granted the lands of Dunolly to the MacDougalls, lands which were forfeited to the Crown after the 1715 Jacobite Rising. But the MacDougalls did not 'come out' for Bonnie Prince Charlie in 1745 and their lands were returned. According to Seton Gordon, the chief's wife made it impossible for him to maintain the old allegiance by taking drastic action – she kept him safely at home by upsetting a pot of boiling water over his feet.

The road to Dunolly passes a still older token of Oban's past. It is a tall stone standing over the shore which legend tells us that Fingal – hero of the Ossianic cycle – used to tie up his hound, Bran. The stone is called in Gaelic 'Clach-na-Choin', the dog's pillar. History, on the other hand, suggests that it served as a tethering post for their hounds when the Lords of the Isles visited the Lords of Lorne.

Oban retains its links with the past, but it remains in essence a Victorian town, crowned – and crowned is the word – by the edifice known as McCaig's Tower. But tower is a misnomer – the astonishing structure on the hill overlooking the town is no less than a replica of the Colosseum at Rome. The Georgians built their follies; the Victorians combined folie de grandeur with philanthropic enterprise. So it was that in 1897 work was started on what was to bring together a family mausoleum with a museum, art gallery and a central tower one-hundred feet high. The scheme was interrupted by

McCaig's death and, fortunately perhaps, was
never completed. The garden and look-out
platform now provide fine views and in its
time, McCaig's Tower may have served part
of its original purpose in reducing the epide-
mic of unemployment which followed the
Clearances. Deprived of their small holdings,
many of the crofters moved to the more prosperous south in search of work. An age-old
way of life was being destroyed: what Bonnie
Prince Charlie's defeat at Culloden had
started, the Clearances came close to finishing
off.

The population of Oban is about 7,500, still
a small town, which nevertheless manages to

Oban Pier

accommodate the yearly influx of tourists, many of whom claim descent from these very victims of the sheep farming policies who found a new livelihood overseas, in America, Canada or Australia.

As Easter approaches, Oban takes on a new life, with the harbour as its main centre of activity. Yachts and other pleasure craft crowd the moorings, where pride of place is given to the Caledonian MacBrayne ferries, now running full steam ahead. Ships on the two-hourly service to Craignure, and the longer crossing direct to Tobermory itself, are packed with tourists eager to explore Mull. There are day long trips for those want-

17

ing a sight of islands further off, Coll and Tiree, and out at sea beyond the Firth of Lorn, Colonsay. Oban is also the starting point for Barra and South Uist, across the Minch, at the southern end of the Outer Hebrides. Meanwhile, the daily local routine goes calmly on: the fishing boats waiting for the tide swing at anchor and on the quay, there is the usual orderly jumble of nets and tackle. From Mull, the morning ferries land the island's residents, come to shop in Oban, which remains very much the metropolis of the district. The bustle continues throughout the day. Then, on a fine evening, as the last ferries draw in and excursion buses return from the hinterland, there is a chance to see a West Coast spectacular: a golden sun setting the sky on fire as it sinks below the hills. As night settles in, the lights in the town go out and the tall grey houses sleep under their slate roofs.

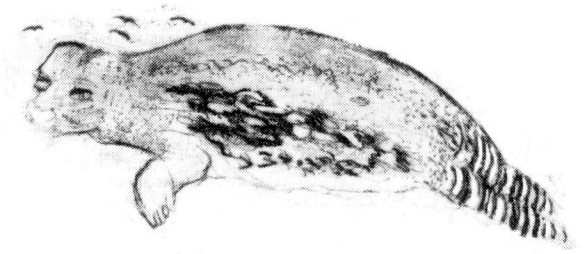

II
Lords of the Isle

'There are three Castles in the Isle, to wit, the Castle of Duart, situated on the East, built upon a Rock, the East side is surrounded by the Sea. This was the Seat of Sir John Mack-Lean, Head of the antient Family of the Mack-Leans; and is now ... become the Duke of Argyle's Property, by the Forfeiture of Sir John. Some Miles further on the West Coast, stands the Castle of Moy, at the head of Lochbuy, and is the seat of Mack-Lean of Lochbuy. There is an old Castle at Aros in the middle of the Island, now in ruins.' Martin also noted the presence of 'old forts, here called Dunns, supposed to have been built by the Danes'. Ruined duns and the remains of more elaborate fortifications known as brochs are scattered throughout the West Highlands and the Hebrides. In essence, they were defence posts from which watch was kept for raiders approaching by sea or land; in the bigger ones, crofters from the vicinity could take temporary refuge till the danger was over.

Duart and Aros and Lochbuy are all indicated on the map Martin provided to accompany his 'Description of the Western Islands of Scotland'. But history was not his prime purpose, as he makes clear in his dedication to Prince George of Denmark. For Martin, himself a Scotsman born on the Isle of Skye, was well acquainted with the poverty prevalent in the islands, and he deplored it. He was convinced that though the Hebrides and the Highlands were backward, they had great commercial potential. Having complained that they were but little known or considered, 'owing to their great distance from the Imperial Seat, rather than their want of Native Worth', he adds firmly that 'by Improvement (they) might render a considerable Accession and Riches to the Crown, as appears by a Scheme annexed to the following Treatise'. This scheme was based on observations made during journeys throughout the Hebrides, from Lewis south to Arran and Bute, during the last two decades of the seventeenth century. As a glance at the Table of Contents shows, its range is enormous for all was grist to Martin's mill.

Information is provided about rivers and fountains and springs, and the qualities of their water; about the bait used to catch trout and eels; about corals and fresh-water pearls; about the arrival of St Columba, the habits of whales, cattle disease, the diversity of sea fowl, the making of bread from barley and oats, the use of charmel root to cure a hangover, and a great deal more besides. 'A Description of the Western Islands of Scotland' came out in 1703; a second edition followed in 1716. It was the first account of the Western Islands to appear in print and still provides an excellent introduction to the Hebrides and their folkways three hundred years ago. It is not always easy to disentangle fact from fancy in Martin's jumble of findings, for he was enough of a man of his time to accept what he was told however improbable. Lore and legend mingle freely with scientific observation, but Martin is always conscientious and astonishingly accurate when he is at his main business of charting the dangerous seaways and recommending the safest harbours.

Coll, for instance, is praised for 'the Cod and Ling (which) abound on the Coast of this Isle, and are of a larger Size there than in the adjacent Isles or the Continent'. But although the short chapter on Coll is of no more than four paragraphs, Martin finds room for a warning against the 'Train of Rocks, call'd the Carn of Coll; they reach about half a League from the Shore, and are remarkable for their Fatality to Sea-faring Men, of which there are several late Instances.'

His description of Mull is equally painstaking: 'The Isle of Mull lies on the West Coast, opposite to Lochaber, Swoonard, and Moydort. It is divided from these by a narrow Channel, not exceeding half-a-League in breadth; the Isle is twenty-four Miles long, from South to North, and as many in breadth from East to West. A South-East Moon causes high Tide here. This Isle is in the Sheriffdom of Argyle; the Air here is temperately cold and moist; the fresh Breezes that blow from the Mountains do in some measure qualify it . . . there is a great Ridge of Mountains about the middle of the Isle, one of them very high, and therefore call'd Bein Vore (Ben More), i.e. a great Mountain . . . There are some Bays, and Places for anchorage about the Isle. The Bay of Duart on the East Side, and to the North of the Castle of that Name, is reckoned a safe Anchoring-place and frequented by Strangers. Lochbuy on the opposite West Side, is but an indifferent Harbour, yet Vessels go into it for Herring.'

On modern maps, Mull appears less square and squat than on Martin's, which, incidentally, makes no mention of Tobermory since it was then no more than a huddle of mud huts and 'black' houses on the hillside. And one statistic escaped him: the island's coast is so deeply indented, especially on the West, that it measures three-hundred miles. In other respects, much of what Martin has to say still applies and, certainly, 'Strangers' continue to visit Duart Castle.

The castle first appears as the ferry from Oban rounds the north end of Kerrera and passes the legendary Lady's Rock on its way to Craignure. High on the east promontory of Duart Bay, the castle stands foursquare to the sea which surrounds it on three sides and has defended it for some seven centuries. Complete with its keep and mighty stone walls rising straight from the rock, its dungeons and its battlements, it is much as it was when it was the great stronghold of Clan Maclean. But what we now see is mainly the result of patient and devoted work: the castle was reconstructed before the First World War by the twenty-sixth chief – and tenth Baronet – Sir Fitzroy Maclean, who lived on till the

Duart Castle

age of 102 to enjoy his achievement in rebuilding what had become little more than a ruin. Duart Castle did not fall to an invader, nor was it destroyed by enemy hands – it was the victim of politics. Backing the losing side led to the forfeiture of the Maclean estates and left their castle at the mercy of the weather and the relentless erosion of more than a century of neglect.

The history of Clan Maclean, of which there are several branches, starts in the thirteenth century when the Macleans became one of the most powerful vassals of the Mac-Donalds, who were themselves descended from a younger son of Somerled, Lord of the Isles – a title the MacDonalds were later to assume. Though himself of Scandinavian descent and allied by marriage to King Olaf the Red, Somerled helped fight off the Norse Invaders, whose dominance of the Hebridean waters came to an end in 1263 when King Haakon of Norway was defeated at the battle of Largs. His troops destroyed and his fleet scattered, King Haakon himself died in the Orkneys during his retreat. The progenitor of the Macleans of Mull, Gillean of the Battle-axe, fought at Largs, a battle historically important since it led to peace between Norway and Scotland and removed for good the threat of the Nordic presence.

This was the time when the clans of the Highlands and Islands grew in strength and importance, ruling their domains with what amounted to regal powers and free to choose their own allegiances.

The Norsemen were defeated, but with the Norman invasion, there was now another enemy to face – the English. The Mac-Donalds and the Macleans supported King Robert the Bruce, himself a Norman – his name was Robert de Brus – who, ironically, succeeded in uniting the Scots and leading them to victory over the English forces in 1314 at the decisive battle of Bannockburn, near Stirling. But the men from the Islands who had first followed The Bruce opposed his Stuart successors, who had come to the Crown through the marriage of Walter the Steward to Robert Bruce's daughter, Marjorie. Nearly a hundred years later, in 1411, another Maclean leader, nicknamed Red Hector of the Battles, fell at Harlaw. This time, Macleans and MacDonalds faced Stuart forces; the battle was savage and the help they had been promised by their English allies never came. The history of Scotland stormed on, and in the following century, Lachlan Maclean of Duart was killed in 1513 at Flodden. This most famous, and disastrous of battles, fought in border country just south of the Tweed, engaged the Scottish forces under their King, James the Fourth, defending the Auld Alliance with France, against the better armed troops of his brother-in-law, Henry the Eighth; it ended in a massacre. King James was killed, with nine earls and fourteen of his nobles, bishops and dignitaries fell on Flodden Field, clan chiefs and their followers were wiped out. A fine ballad commemorates their end:

'I've heard them lilting, at the ewe
  milking,
Lasses a'lilting, before dawn of day;
But now they are moaning, on ilka green
  loaning;
The flowers of the forest are a' wede
  away.'

It was the death, also on the battlefield, of
another chief named Hector which provided
the Macleans with their war cry. Eight
hundred Maclean clansmen took part in the
battle of Inverkeithing on the northern shore
of the Firth of Forth. It was fought in 1651
during Cromwell's attempt to invade Scotland while it was in the grip of its own
religious wars of the Covenant. The fighting
was deadly – of the Maclean contingent, there
were only four survivors. Among the dead
were seven brothers, who rallied to the
defence of their Chief, Sir Hector, each crying
in turn as he fell, 'Another for Hector'.

The fortunes of the Stuarts, meanwhile,
were on the decline. The marriage of Walter
the Steward to the Bruce's daughter had
brought them to the throne; recalling the circumstances, King James the Fifth, father of
Mary Queen of Scots is quoted as saying: 'It
came with a lass and it will gang with a lass.'
His prophecy was not fulfilled, for Mary's
son, James the Sixth, and First of England,
eventually ruled over both kingdoms. But the
Stuart cause was as good as lost when William
of Orange was invited to England to take
over after the Revolution of 1688 which sent

James the Second into exile. Yet James retained his supporters in England as well as in Scotland – toasts were drunk in secret to 'The King over the Water'. And when William died after being thrown when his horse stumbled on a molehill, there were toasts too for 'the little gentleman in black velvet'. Under his successor, Queen Anne, a Treaty of Union with Scotland was signed: it only emphasised the great divide between the Lowlands and Highlanders, who were confirmed in their old allegiance to the Stuarts. With the arrival of George the First, the Risings began. In his History of the English-Speaking Peoples, Sir Winston Churchill described the first of the Georgian kings as he landed in the late summer of 1714: 'Here on English soil stood an unprepossessing figure, an obstinate and humdrum martinet with dull brains and coarse tastes. . . . As a ruler of men, he had shown no quickening ability or generosity of spirit. Yet the rigidity of his mind was relieved by a slow shrewdness and a brooding commonsense. The British throne was no easy inheritance for a foreign figure. King George took it up grudgingly, and it was ungraciously that he played his allotted part. He owed his crown to the luck of circumstance, but he never let it slip from his grasp.' The Fifteen, which saw James the Second's son, James Edward, proclaimed King James the Seventh (and Third) at Braemar, was marked by the battle of Sheriffmuir where Maclean of Duart led the charge, crying: 'Here stands Maclean for King James.

God bless Maclean and King James.' The battle was indecisive, and the final blow to hopes of a Stuart restoration was dealt by James Edward himself when, at the end of the following year, he slipped away from Scotland back into exile. It was left to his son, Charles Edward, to make a final attempt to restore the Stuart fortunes. His campaign came to an end on Drumossie Moor, outside Inverness, at the battle more generally known as Culloden. It was fought on the 16th of April 1746. Again the Macleans took part, along with the MacDonalds, the men of Clan Chattan, Camerons, Stewarts of Appin, MacGregors, MacLachlans – a roll call of famous clan names. The massacre of the ill-equipped Highlanders, followed by the butchery of the wounded and prisoners by the Duke of Cumberland's men, have gone down to history; the subsequent escape of Bonnie Prince Charlie, to legend.

The Prince took to the heather with a price of thirty thousand pounds on his head. This was indeed a king's ransom, worth at least half a million pounds nowadays. It speaks highly of the Scottish tradition of hospitality that he was never betrayed. For six months or so, he moved across Scotland pursued by the Redcoats and protected by the invincible loyalty of his adherents till, on a dark September dawn, he boarded a French ship, which slipped safely out of Loch Nan Uamh, and followed his father into exile, the last of the royal Stuarts to set foot on his ancestral soil. By this time, the most famous of his associates in the final stages of his escape, Flora MacDonald, was already under arrest and on her way to London – she was released the following year under the Act of Amnesty. Others suffered a worse fate – clansmen who had merely followed their chiefs had their houses burnt down as troops scoured the moors for the royal fugitive; hundreds were transported; many died in the prison hulks at Tilbury; among the Jacobite leaders, old Lord Lovat was taken to the Tower of London and beheaded; most of the Highland and Island leaders lost their lands by forfeiture.

After two Rebellions, as London called the risings, in less than forty years, the government was taking no more risks: fierce laws were passed aimed at dismantling clan loyalties. And with them went much of the old way of life. During a year of cruel reprisals, Acts of Parliament were passed disarming the Highlanders and – a shrewd blow at the clan system – banning Highland dress. Under the Disclothing Act, it was a penal offence to wear, 'the Philabeg, or little Kilt, Trowse, Shoulder-Belts or any Part whatsoever of what peculiarly belongs to the Highland Garb.' To what extent either the Disarming Act or the new laws governing dress were implemented remains open to question: such notorious incidents in the continuing history of clan feuds as the Appin Murder show that plenty of cold steel remained hidden on the moor, and guns and ammunition, too. And there were many ways of circumventing the suppression of the plaid – it is said that rather than discard the large tartan cloak which, belted, turned into a kilt by day and provided a blanket by night, canny crofters sewed it up to form a sort of baggy pantaloons. Historians still disagree about how much value, apart from convenience, the croftsmen attached to their dress.

However, by the time the Act was repealed in 1785, the kilt was no longer in use for the old weavers had died and the traditional patterns with them. A revival took place in 1822 when, with Sir Walter Scott acting as master of ceremonies, George the Fourth entered Edinburgh, his vast bulk swathed in a kilt; Queen Victoria, in love with Balmoral and all things Scottish started a new fashion of the wearing of tartans in all their complexity. The true significance of Highland dress may be lost; of its antiquity, there is no doubt. The historian of the clans, Robert Bain, gives the Macleod hunting tartan as an instance. With narrow stripes of white and black running down and across a background of dark forest green, it was registered in 1587 as part of a feu duty of sixty ells of cloth when the heir of Duart, Hector Maclean, was granted land on Islay. It is thought to be the oldest tartan for which there is documentary evidence.

The drama of Bonnie Prince Charlie's flight was played out many miles north of Mull. But distance meant nothing – he was as loyally defended and fondly remembered there as elsewhere. The ballad calling for his return 'O'er the sea to Skye' is perhaps the best known in the Jacobite canon; Mull had the 'Maclean's Welcome' to offer him.

'Come o'er the stream, Charlie, dear
   Charlie, brave Charlie,
Come o'er the stream, Charlie, and dine
   with Maclean;
And though you be weary, we'll make
   your heart cheery,
And welcome our Charlie and his loyal
   train.
We'll bring down the track deer, we'll
   bring down the black steer,
The lamb from the brechan, and doe from
   the glen;
The salt sea we'll harry, and bring to our
   Charlie
The cream from the bothy, and curd from
   the pen.'

– a banquet which was to end with 'the wine that is red/ to drink to your sire and his friend, the Maclean'.

But there was a heavy price to pay for sporting the 'White Cockade', emblem of the Jacobites, and in common with many other chiefs, the Macleans paid it in full. The sixteenth and seventeenth centuries had seen a steady increase in their power and influence; their allegiance to the Stuart marked their decline. Sir John Maclean's estates were forfeited in 1691 under William of Orange and eventually passed into the hands of the clan's arch-enemy, Campbell of Argyll. Duart Castle was abandoned, left to stand unten-

anted on the black crag from which it gets its name (Dubh Ard: the black height).

Another of the castles Martin Martin listed, Castle Moy built in the 14th century, stands on the shore of the deep bay of Loch Buie. It is within easy reach of Duart – by a side road which branches off the main road (A849) through the Ross of Mull to Iona to hug the northern bank of Loch Spelve. By the side of Lochbuie House in its belt of trees, its battlements emerging from the ivy which cloaks its powerful walls, it was the ancient seat of Clan MacLaine, whose ancestors were closely related to the Macleans of Duart. The MacLaines received their lands – some of the most

fertile on Mull – in the days of the Lords of
the Isles and the grant was confirmed to their
chief John Og by King James the Fourth. But
the MacLaines lost them for a time through a
feud with the Duart Macleans, in which John
Og was killed with two of his sons. The
third, Malcolm, who was still an infant, was
taken to safety in Ireland, and later returned
to recapture his castle at Lochbuie, with the
help, it is said, of the old woman who had
nursed him during his childhood in exile.
Later, the MacLaines became strong supporters of the Stuarts and suffered
accordingly.

Castle Moy has one peculiarity – a flooded

dungeon where prisoners had the choice of drowning or crouching on the narrow top of a rock which stands above the waters. Their level, nine feet deep, had probably receded, however, when late in the eighteenth century, the Laird of Lochbuy imprisoned 'several persons' in it. The case caused a stir when it came up in court in Edinburgh, with James Boswell's father, Lord Auchinlech as one of the judges. Lochbuy was heavily fined, but remained impenitent. Johnson and Boswell spent their last night on Mull as his guests, and Boswell found there was no shaking his belief in his hereditary right to administer summary justice on his own domain. He described the laird as 'a bluff, comely, noisy old gentleman, proud of his hereditary consequence and a very hearty and hospitable landlord'. As a host, however, he had his limitations – he was quite unaware of the identity of Dr Johnson, asking his famous guest, 'Are you of the Johnstons of Glencro, or of Ardnamurchan?' Perhaps for the first time ever, Johnson was speechless, and it was left to Boswell to explain that his friend was Johnson, not Johnston, and an Englishman to boot. For his part, Johnson mentions the incident only briefly, and has nothing to say about another of his host's faux pas: the offer of so 'vulgar' a dish as cold sheep's head for breakfast next day. But he has plenty to say about Castle Moy and its dungeon and the customs of ancient times, when: 'the traveller, whoever he might be, coming to the fortified habitation of a chieftain, would, probably, have been interrogated from the battlements, admitted with caution at the gate, introduced to a petty Monarch, fierce with habitual hostility, and vigilant with ignorant suspicion; who, according to his general temper, or accidental humour, would have seated a stranger as his guest at table, or as a spy confined him in the dungeon.'

Johnson and Boswell had been brought to Lochbuy by Sir Allan Maclean, the twenty-second chief of Duart, with whom they had been staying on Inch Kenneth, the small island off the west coast at the mouth of Loch Na Keal. Landing from Mull, Johnson described it as: '. . . about a mile long, and perhaps half a mile broad, remarkable for pleasantness and fertility. It is verdant and grassy, and fit both for pasture and tillage; but it has no trees.' Boswell echoed him: 'Inchkenneth is a pretty little island . . . all good land.' What neither of them remarked on is the magnificent view across the Gribun flats to the high cliffs which end the westerly slopes of Ben More. But landscape had not yet come into its own, and Johnson was more taken up with the strange contrast between his host and his lodgings. 'Romance', the Doctor writes, 'does not often exhibit a scene that strikes the imagination more than this little desert in these depths of Western obscurity, occupied not by a gross herdsman, or amphibious fisherman, but by a gentleman and two ladies, of high birth, polished manners, and elegant conversation, who, in a habitation raised not very far above the ground, but furnished with unexpected neatness and convenience, practise all the kindness of hospitality, and refinement of courtesy.' He added this tribute to his host: 'Though by the misconduct of his ancestors, most of the extensive territory, which would have descended to him, has been alienated, he still retains much of the dignity and authority of his birth.' In addition to keeping a good table, Sir Allan had a collection of books in his cottage. 'What else is necessary,' said Dr Johnson, 'to make his house pleasant.'

As was the custom in days when roads were bad and inns, where they existed, worse, travellers could always count on the hospitality of the local lairds and their kin. So far we have met the MacLeans and Sir Allan's brother-in-law, the Laird of Lochbuie entertaining Johnson and Boswell; they were to get to know one other of Mull's ancient families, the MacQuarries of Ulva. Through their connection with the elusive Clan Alpine, the MacQuarries may have some claim to royal blood. But what consequence they once had they lost when their chief, Allan MacQuarrie and most of the clan were killed at Inverkeithing. Five years after Johnson and Boswell visited the MacQuarries on Ulva, the last recognised clan chief, Lachlan, who lived to the age of one hundred and three, was forced to sell what was left of his lands. The name, however, still means a lot in Australia, where a descendant, Major-General Lachlan MacQuarrie, as governor of New South Wales, laid out the city of Sydney. And the General has his monument on Mull – a mausoleum in extensive grounds at the head of Loch Ba.

When he arrived on Ulva, on the 17th of October 1773, Dr Johnson, for his part, was in no doubt as to the family's status. It was 'a clan not powerful nor numerous, but of antiquity, which most other families are content to reverence'. Boswell adds that the Mac-Quarries had held Ulva for nine hundred years. In this 'mean' house, the travellers found – as so often before on their tour – a host 'intelligent, polite and much a man of the world'. A further contrast between the family and their surroundings was provided when Johnson retired for the night. It had been raining and the earthen floor of the bedroom he shared with Boswell, having neither boards nor carpet, he found himself standing barefoot in the 'mire'.

Debt destroyed the MacQuarries; politics were the MacDougall's undoing. After the battle of Bannockburn, their estates on Mull were forfeited and handed over to King Robert the Bruce's ally, Angus Og MacDonald, King of the Isles. These included the castle of Aros which was once part of an elaborate system of defence, covering Ardnamuchan and Morvern and down the Sound of Mull, reaching to Loch Aline and across to Duart at the head of the Firth of Lorn. Under James the First (Sixth), a viceregal court was held at Aros, where in 1608, a trick was played on the Highland chiefs. They were invited to assemble there, then taken to a banquet held on the royal ship which was stand-

Aros Castle

ing off-shore. Once aboard, they were made prisoner and conveyed to Edinburgh where they were not released until they had signed the Statutes of Iona, which reformed island rule.

The direct line of MacDougall of Lorn came to an end in the 14th century, when John of Lorn died without male issue. Through his daughters, his lands passed to the Stewarts of Lorn, along with the castles of Dunolly and Dunstaffnage.

The ruins of Aros castle stand north of Salen Bay at the head of Glen Aros. The river of the same name runs inland into Loch Frisa, which is bordered by the fine woods of Salen Forest, much of it planted (in 1925) with pine, larch and spruce and maintained by the Forestry Commission. The by-road running through the Glen comes out at Dervaig on the West coast, and the detour is well worth while. But tourists with limited time may prefer to carry on north along the coast road (A848) to the island's capital – and, to many, its showpiece – Tobermory.

III

Spanish Gold and
Silver Darlings

On one of his many journeys north of the
border, the writer, S. P. B. Mais, made acquaintance with Mull by sea. In his book 'I
Return to Scotland', he writes, 'For weeks we
had looked out from Oban on the sun setting
each night more majestically beyond Kerrera,
behind the sugar-loaf of Ben More, to leave
the magic unexplored island of Mull
shrouded deeper and deeper in mystery. Then
at last we could bear it no longer. We started
off to encircle the island.' Crossing the Firth
of Lorn into the Sound of Mull, he describes a
landscape of mountains, 'Ben More recedes
and other peaks come into the foreground,
Sgurr Dearg, Beinn Talaidh and Dun da
Ghaoithe all three about 2,500 feet.' Then
came Duart Castle and, across the Sound,
'Ardtornish Castle, Loch Aline, and the hills
of Morvern away to the North.' Soon after,
another view of Mull, with 'the green pleas-
ance of Salen', and the road winding north
towards Tobermory. Tobermory, he says, is
well worth interrupting one's journey for 'it
has a character of its own. The old part lies
hidden among trees on the steep hillside, but
there is a long row of houses, shops, hotels,
and churches standing along the waterfront'.
Oddly enough, Mais does not mention an
unexpected feature of Tobermory's main

street – in startling contrast to the sometimes grim grey stone of most Scottish towns, here the houses are brightly painted, geranium and ochre, royal blue and navy, black and white and cream, and violet. So are many of the small craft bobbing up and down in the bay. The pretty sight struck another modern mariner, Neil Gunn. 'With the sun shining, the bay, tricked out in wooded slopes and shimmering yachts, looked a lovely sight, and like a dancing holiday.'

The history of Tobermory reaches far back into the past; understandably, since from the earliest times it has generally been considered one of the safest anchorages in these parts. The wooded hill behind it provided a vantage point, as well as timber. In addition, there was a well – which gives Tobermory its name, St Mary's Well in the Gaelic. Nowadays, Tobermory houses some eight hundred people, about a third of the island's entire population. But the little township did not come into any particular prominence until Elizabethan times, when the still unexplained sinking in the bay of a ship from the Spanish Armada gave rise to persistent rumours of lost treasure. After its defeat in 1588, the Spanish fleet was scattered and blown northwards, and many of the ships, hoping for refuge in Ireland, sought a way through the Hebrides. One of them, the *Florida*, a galleon from (now Dubrovnik) Ragusa, put into Tobermory in search of provisions. There are several versions of what happened next: according to one, Maclean of Duart gave the

Spanish supplies. But payment was slow in coming, and the Maclean factor, sent aboard to collect the monies, was made prisoner and the ship weighed anchor. In revenge, he succeeded in making his way to the powder magazine and blew it up. He made good his escape before the ship foundered and was lost with its entire crew and a cargo of gold and silver coin. In another account, the Spanish paid their debt by lending Maclean a hundred Spanish troops to pursue a feud against the Macleans of Coll. The campaign was a bloody one and it seems that, while fighting alongside the clansmen, the Spaniards let slip the secret of their ship's cargo – some say she was carrying the whole Armada's treasure chest. So she was sunk in Tobermory bay for the sake of her ducats and doubloons.

A more fanciful version of the story involves witchcraft: Maclean's wife became aware of the frequent visits her husband was paying to the galleon and surmising it was for the sake of a pretty Spanish lady he had met on board, called on the dark powers to dispose of the ship and her attractions. The official account, however, exculpates the Macleans entirely: according to this, the galleon was blown up by a Scottish spy who got wind of the treasure on board the ship and sent her to the bottom. Even her name is in dispute – she has been identified as the *San Juan de Sicilia* as well as the *Florencia*, though she is now generally accepted as the *Florida*.

When Martin was on Mull, the sinking of

the *Florida* was still being discussed. His account, close to the current one, runs as follows: 'One of the Ships of the Spanish Armada, called the *Florida*, perished in this (Tobermory) Bay, having been blown up by one Smallett of Dunbarton in the Year 1588. There was a great Sum of Gold and Mony on board the Ship, which disposed the Earl of Argyle and some Englishmen to attempt the Recovery of it; but how far the latter succeeded in his Enterprize is not generally known; only that some Pieces of Gold, and Mony, and a Golden Chain was taken out of her. I have seen some fine brass Cannon, some Pieces of Eight, Teeth, Beads and Pins that had been taken out of that Ship.'

Attempts continued to be made to reach what remains of the *Florida* – in one mounted in 1955 by the Duke of Argyll, navy divers went down. Various objects were recovered – brass cannon, swords and small arms, silver goblets, some coin. But many people believe that a fortune in gold lies eleven fathoms deep encrusted in the sea bed.

The search for another sort of treasure – shoals of silver herring and great catches of cod – was to prove equally elusive. Martin's work on the natural resources of the Hebrides came at the wrong time and his appeal for investment fell on deaf ears. The Wars of the Spanish Succession were being fought when Martin was sailing through the Western Isles, and England had no ships to spare, nor timber to build them; the second edition of his 'Description' came out in 1716 just as the First

Rising was being defeated, and this was not the moment for England to come to the rescue of the rebellious Highlands. By the end of the century, however, the political climate had changed, and the newly-founded Society for Extending the Fisheries was ready to adopt John Knox's suggestions. These included purpose-built fishing stations to house the seamen it intended to recruit. Ullapool went up north of the Great Glen on the shores of Loch Broom; on Skye, there is Stein by the sea-shore in Vaternish. The Society's purpose was part philanthropic, part commercial; it appealed to some of the great landlords who followed suit in attempting to develop local fisheries. Thus, the Earl of Seaforth went to work on rebuilding Stornoway on Lewis, adding a pier and assembling a small fleet of busses – as the herring boats were called. And under the aegis of the Duke of Argyll, the little town of Inveraray below the castle was extended along Loch Fyne. The main feature of these new towns was a solid pier where the fishing boats could now tie up instead of being dragged on to the open beach to unload their catch. As well as the neat stone cottages, there were also church buildings, an inn, a school house. This early experiment in town planning seemed both far-sighted and practical. But it failed, and no-one quite knows why.

Many blamed the native indolence of the Hebridean crofters. The rhyme known as the 'Crofter's Prayer' satirises their alleged attitude to the day's work:

'Oh that the peats should cut themselves,
The fish slump on the shore,
And that we all should lie in bed
For aye and evermore.'

But Dr Johnson knew better: in his day, he was perhaps alone in recognising the terror, all too often justified, that the open seas held for landsmen, and particularly for their wives. He wrote: 'If it were always practical to fish, these Islands could never be in much danger from famine; but unhappily in winter, when other provisions fail, the seas are commonly too rough for nets, or boats.' Equally to the point these nets and boats had to be bought, and few crofters had money enough to acquire them outright. The most enterprising engaged their catch against the eventual ownership of their vessel, and hired their nets and other tackle by the same means. The deal was as precarious for the creditor as for the would-be fisherman he backed. Few of the fishing boats that set out so gallantly exceeded fourteen or seventeen feet in length; not many had sails. Masted ships with a full complement of sails were far beyond the average crofter's means, or his navigational skills. So most of the newly-made mariners rowed out to drop their nets in sea lochs and inshore waters. Only a few who were able to rig up a sail ventured further out into the open seas in the hope of hooking ling or cod, the most highly prized of the catch. With neither maps nor even compass to guide them, recognising landmarks only by hearsay, they were at the

mercy of the Atlantic's sudden storms and furious seas. Sometimes, their efforts were rewarded; too often, they were lost, over-turned or dashed to pieces on the cliffs and skerries that abound in Hebridean waters. And during the Napoleonic Wars, another danger lurked for any boat that strayed from the little fishing fleet – an encounter with a naval patrol ship which would intercept it and press-gang its crew.

For protection, the sailors had little but their native wit – and prayer. A superb example is to be found in the Gaelic epic known as the Birlinn of Clanranald. Springing from oral tradition, it was written down by a local man, Alexander MacDonald, who was born round about the year 1700 in Ardnamurchan where he spent most of his life as a schoolmaster. The poem describes a journey by sea from South Uist to Belfast Lough in Northern Ireland, during which the open galley, taking off from Loch Eynort slipped south between Coll and Tiree, passed west of the Ross of Mull, just avoiding the Torran Rocks, went through the Sound of Islay and crossed to Carrickfergus. In the translation by the modern poet Hugh MacDiarmid (provided by Elizabeth Bray in her 'Discovery of the Hebrides'), it starts with the customary 'ship blessing':

'God bless the craft of Clanranald
When brangled first with the brine,
Himself and his heroes hurling;
The pick of the human line!

The blessing of holy Triune
On the fury of the air;
The sea's ruggedness smoothed away
Ease us to our haven there!

Father who fashioned the ocean
And winds that from all points roll,
Bless our lean ship and her heroes,
Keep her and her whole crew whole!

Holy Ghost, be you our helmsman
To steer the course that is right.
You know every port under Heaven,
We cast ourselves on your sleight.'

Should prayer fail, there was a vast body of superstition to fall back on. Many words were banned at sea – no reference could be

47

made to salmon, pigs, hares and rabbits or rats. The use of the word 'rock', understandably, was taboo – it was referred to as a 'hard'. A common belief affected the sailor's clothing – nothing dyed with crotal should be worn at sea because it was held that this widely used rock lichen came from the sea and would return to it. In some parts, a similar embargo applied to seal-skin. By taking such precautions, you might avoid bad luck; and there were means of bringing good luck, too: by turning the boat sunwise (deasil) before setting out and by tying a piece of the magic rowan tree to the tackle. Sometimes, elder was used instead. Other old customs concerned the fish itself – Martin came across the practice of throwing back any herring of unusual size in the belief that it might be the King Herring, for it was held that if the King were to die and leave them leaderless, the whole school would scatter. Martin also noted that herring were thought to fear blood – if a fight broke out on shore and blood was shed, the herring would leave the coast. But it seems that neither prayer nor the occult powers could prevent such common accidents as being followed by dogfish – 'the dogs' they were called – who would tear their way through the nets and savage the catch. Or meeting with a whale on the look-out for fish falling through the meshes: it would not attack a boat but could easily overturn it in its mighty wake.

That anyone who was not bred to it should elect to follow so precarious a trade may seem astonishing, but once the Clearances were under way, the dispossessed had little choice. The alternative was emigration. Sometimes, there was good money to be earned from fishing for profit – from the bounty the government paid for a cran of big, sound herring – and paid work for the women in gutting the herring ready for salting. On the other hand, a job which took the men abroad meant neglecting the croft. Much of the work was too heavy for women in the days when the cas-chrom, or foot-plough, was the only tool available to turn over land strewn with boulders and knotted with the tough roots of heather and gorse. But in the long run, it was lack of planning as much as anything that defeated the fishing trade which eventually lost out to foreign competition. The demand was there, but not the mechanism to meet it. It was, for instance, almost impossible for curers in the isolated stations in the far north to get salt delivered in small enough quantities, and the price of salt itself remained far too high: it rose again in 1801 and the tax was not abolished until 1825. There were too many middlemen. The curers themselves became part of the community, on shore when the fleet came in and present as the barrels filled up with the glittering catch. But the Glasgow merchant who bought it was as remote from the Hebridean fishermen as the German burgher enjoying the delicacy of fresh herring with spring vegetables. Much of the Baltic trade was lost to Norway; the profitable sale to Jamaica of the cheapest fish, to

Tobermory

feed the negroes on the plantations, went with the abolition of slavery. All these factors helped to put an end to the great fisheries experiment – roofless cottages on the shore and upturned boats rotting away bear witness to its decline. It has been argued that it was the unpredictable migratory habit of the herring, still unexplained, which dealt it a final blow. A loch or stretch of coast which year after year filled each spring with herring would suddenly be deserted as the fish moved on, and a single season missed could spell ruin to the fishermen. It seems, however, that it was Bowman who held the answer: 'Before experiments of this kind can succeed', he

wrote, 'a great change in the dispositions and habits of the people must be effected.'

Bowman reached this conclusion during a visit to Tobermory. He was well aware, had indeed experienced, some of the dangers of the local waters. As he found out, 'these seas are difficult of navigation, even in the day, without most skillful and experienced pilotage, on account of the stormy currents, heaving swells, and points of rock that lurk below'. Even those who knew the coast best could meet their death at sea. Thus, the young Laird of Col who had entertained Dr Johnson and Boswell during their travels in 1773 and assisted their passage from his island

to Mull was drowned a few years later during the short passage from Ulva to Inch Kenneth.

Of Tobermory itself, this is what Bowman has to say: 'A village lying a little to the east of the north point of Mull, and consisting of two portions, the lower, modern and stretching along a pier, the upper consisting only of some mean huts perched upon a perpendicular hill above it. . . . Tobermory is so called from a spring in the neighbourhood which has the reputation of possessing sanative qualities . . . this village was built under the auspices of the Society for the Encouragement of the Fisheries in 1789, but from various causes the project has failed; and the place, though lying in the direct track of the numerous vessels which pass from the more southern ports to the northern countries of Europe, does not consist of more than thirty houses, and perhaps twice as many small turf huts.'

This was written in 1825 and, given the 'mud huts', Tobermory has changed surprisingly little in the two hundred years and more since it was built up into a designated fishing station. Though it ranks as the island's 'capital', it is still a small town, a very small town indeed. Yachts and small craft have replaced the old fishing boats; the steam packets from Glasgow which covered the Western Isles have given way to 'Cal-Mac' ferries; occasional 'mini-cruise' ships call at the pier and coaches and buses bring in the travellers who once rode or walked across the moor. But so far Tobermory has not given in to any of the excesses of the tourist trade: it has learnt to adapt itself without radically changing its way of life. Tobermory carries on quietly on its steady course, and it is not too difficult to imagine oneself back in the days when Bowman was there. Tourists out for a walk or taking the steep path at the entrance of the main street which leads up into the woods will find the scenery much the same – 'a strong hilly road' over moorland, 'some pretty waterfalls' and the 'fine coppice woods which overlooked the bay and a cliffy glen of great beauty rising in terraces immediately from its edge'. 'Mull', Bowman writes, 'was formerly celebrated for its woods.' His use of the word 'formerly' indicates that in his day

'Mull of the trees' as it had been called was already suffering visibly from the ever-growing demand for timber.

Mull still seems the greenest of all the Hebrides, and well wooded, too. And what is left of the old broad-leaved trees are seen at their best in the vicinity of Tobermory, with beech and elm and ash, silver birch and sycamore, with the spring candles of the chestnut trees and the vivid tangle of the rhododendrons, the woods here are in sharp contrast to the tight ranks of conifers, chiefly Sitka spruce, planted by the Forestry Commission to meet the requirements of the paper industry. There remain on Mull many of the native trees – rowan and juniper, hazelnut and willow and the larches, whose wood is favoured by boat-builders, as well as the Scotch or Caledonian pines which fit the landscape so much better than the stunted regiments of Canadian spruce. In the plantations which are taking over the moors, the trees are planted so tightly that no light filters through and the undergrowth is dead. Naturalists protest that the habitat of bird and beast is being killed off. The whole question is contentious since even the most ardent conservationist cannot ignore the employment opportunities that the Forestry Commission brings to the island.

A similar controversy surrounds the development of another growing industry – fish-farming. Environmentalists complain that the great breeding cages, suspended on the lochs, spoil their natural beauty, and they are joined in their campaign by gourmets who resist all efforts to persuade them that farmed fish and crustaceans have the full flavour of the wild product. However, this twentieth century attempt at exploiting the riches of the Hebridean waters seems set for success – as prices fall and demand increases, salmon and trout and lobster are readily available within reach of modest purses. One unexpected result is that it is becoming difficult to buy 'real' wild smoked salmon in Scotland. Meanwhile, anglers and fly-fishers can still get their sport: salmon and brown trout continue to thrive in lochs and rivers, and shell-fish are caught along the rocky coast. As Martin reported, 'There are several Rivers in this Isle that afford Salmon, and some Rivers abound with the black Muscle that breeds pearl. There are also some fresh-water Lakes that have Trout and Eels.' The pearl-breeding mussels sound like a tall story, but it is a fact that natural pearls are found in Scottish rivers, notably in the Tay, and freshwater pearl fisheries are being set up. When Martin was writing, salmon was so abundant that it was far from being regarded as a delicacy. Though it was highly prized in London, servants in Scottish households tried to make it a condition of their employment that they should not be fed salmon more than twice a week. Wild or cultivated, trout and salmon continue to co-exist. It is still possible to watch salmon leaping within sight of the cages in the river's mouth, and to catch brown trout only a short distance from the man-made nurseries where the rainbow variety are bred.

On Mull, the old and the new sit easily side by side; one slips from one century to another without being aware of the transition. Not far from Tobermory, though accessible to walkers rather than cars, Bloody Bay lies just below Ardmore Point. There a battle was fought in 1480 for the Lordship of the Isles, between Angus Og, bastard son of the titular holder, John, who was supported by the King (James III) and the Macleans. Victory went to Angus – a cruel and vindictive man, historians say – who then ruled the Isles until he was murdered ten years later. More than a hundred years went by before the galleon from the Spanish Armada was sunk outside

Glen More landscape

Tobermory, the next bay down the Sound. Tobermory itself, screened by its old woods, is a well preserved product of the eighteenth century, and the road south back to the main landing stage at Craignure is filled with reminders of the island's long history. All hugger-mugger along the route, cattle graze among the remnants of mysterious stone circles, some of the prehistoric standing stones tumbled on the moor; there are deserted villages of houses burnt out during the Victorian Clearances and a big village school closed down when the people were driven away; there are the medieval ruins of Aros Castle, and the township of Salen, built about 1800 by the man they call 'the father of Australia', General Lachlan Macquarrie. At Pennygown, an ancient cemetery on a mound is crowned by a roofless chapel, dating back to the twelfth century, where black masses are said to have been celebrated. Some say the chapel never had a roof because the witches combined to prevent the stonemasons from finishing their holy work. This particular stretch of the trail, from north to south along the Sound of Mull, ends a mile or so past Craignure, in a complete contrast provided by Torosay Castle – no antique ruin this, but a perfect example of the Victorian style of Gothic Revival, known as Scottish Baronial. Torosay was built in 1858 by David Bryce, the leading exponent of the movement, for the Guthrie family, who still farms its policies and opens both the castle and its grounds to the public. The gardens are famous – they were laid out by Sir Robert Lorimer in a rare example of collaboration between the two eminent Victorians. Covering ten or eleven acres, they include terraces with stone lions and fountains, a water garden and a Japanese one, and an avenue lined with Italian statuary. Bordered by trees, Torosay can be no more than glimpsed from the road: it is best seen from the terrace of Duart Castle across the bay, or from the shore.

A favourite approach to Torosay is by the narrow gauge steam railway that now runs from Craigmure's old pier. All brass and bright colours, the little train was brought into service in 1983. Over the mile or more of its course, it provides beautiful views of the mountains across the water, and with the Castle as its destination, it provides a pretty picture of a more acceptable face of the Victorian age.

IV
On Mull

On the West coast, over by Gribun, the narrow road across the moor drops down and winds its way between the rockface and the sea. The gradient is so steep that few passengers by car or coach are aware that the overhanging cliffs reach up in places to a thousand feet. In any case, most of them are engrossed by the lovely sight of an untidy patchwork of islands spread out before them – Inch Kenneth and Ulva and Gometra, Little Colonsay, Iona and Staffa, the unmistakable Dutchman's Cap in the Treshnish group, and far out to sea Coll and Tiree. But if they are travelling with a local driver, he will not fail to draw their attention inland to a huge boulder which marks the site of an unforgotten tragedy. In 1760, a young couple got married; the celebrations, with all the neighbours and well-wishers dancing to the fiddle, lasted well into the night. Then, the newly marrieds took possession of their home, but they did not survive the landslide that crushed it. By morning, they and their house had been interred under several tons of rock; their bodies were never recovered. Now bushes have broken through the rock and a low wall of stone has been built around their tiny domain. Modern geologists could have warned them that the basalt which makes up the shoreline is extremely unstable – landslips are frequent and the beach itself is littered with chunks of broken rocks. Modern tourists can only wonder at the tiny, insecure cottage in which an 18th century shepherd and his wife looked forward to the future. But such was the way of life that the crofters of Mull were so reluctant to leave. Its meanness, and its insecurity, had already struck Bowman. 'Under the cliffs of Mull', he writes, 'were several of the most diminutive huts we had yet seen, so small indeed, that they might easily have been overlooked among the large masses of rock that lay scattered about them. A person accustomed to the habits and pursuits of civilized society, might justly deem it little better than banishment, were he compelled to lead the amphibious and monotonous life of these secluded beings. . . . Yet notwithstanding all the privations and hardships these poor fishermen are doomed to bear, their attachment to their native rock is insuperable, no advantage afforded by other situations appearing to have any power to create a wish for change.'

Stories without number are told of the Clearances, and there are plenty of contemporary records to back them up. It is impossible to exaggerate the misery inflicted by the policy of replacing men by sheep, nor the petty cruelty that went with it as estates were denuded of their labour. Whole communities – the entire population of a village or a small island – were driven off to find work in the south if they were lucky, to turn vagrant if they were not. Emigration was the obvious solution for those who could afford to pay their passage, or had it paid for them by the kindlier of the landlords who had dispossessed them. But subsidised or not, what is evident is that the crofters did not want to go; what they felt as they waited to board the ships taking them into exile is vividly described in 'Kidnapped'. David Balfour has at last crossed the Ross of Mull – all twenty-seven miles of it – and, reaching Torosay, embarks for the Morvern mainland. (This crossing to Lochaline is now made from Fishnish, further up the coast near Salen.) The weather was bright, the ferry crowded, the passengers taking a turn at the oars and singing Gaelic boat songs, and the crossing was a merry one. 'But there was one melancholy part. In the mouth of Loch Aline we found a great sea-going ship at anchor. . . . As we got a little nearer, it became plain that she was a ship of merchandise; and what still more puzzled me, not only the decks, but the sea-beach also, were quite black with people, and skiffs were continually plying to and fro between them. Yet nearer, and there began to come to our ears a great sound of mourning, the people on board and those on shore crying and lamenting one to another so as to pierce the heart. Then I understood this was an emigrant ship bound for the American colonies. We put the ferry-boat alongside, and the exiles leant over the bulwarks, weeping and reaching out their hands to my fellow passengers, among whom they counted some near friends. . . . At last, the captain of the ship, who seemed near beside himself (and no great wonder) in the midst of this crying and confusion, came to the side and begged us to shear off.... The singer in our boat struck into a melancholy air, which was presently taken up by the emigrants and their friends on the beach, so that it sounded from all sides like a lament for the dying. I saw the tears run down the cheeks of the men and women in the boat, even as they bent at the oars; and the circumstances and the music of the song (which is one called "Lochaber, no more") were highly affecting even to myself.'

It is a common mistake to put the whole blame for the clearances and evictions on to the Victorians – both, the one leading to the other, were being put into operation more than fifty years before Queen Victoria came to the throne. The scene David Balfour describes takes place in 1751. Probably the best known of the laments connected with enforced emigration from the Highlands is the one they call the Canadian Boat Song.

'From the lone shieling of the misty island
Mountains divide us, and the waste of
  seas –
Yet still the blood is strong, the heart is
  Highland
And we in dreams behold the Hebrides!'

It is generally associated with Skye, and has been ascribed to Walter Scott, though its authorship has long been in dispute. 'Lochaber, no more', however, was written by the Scottish poet, Allan Ramsay, who was born in 1686. He turned bookseller, issued collections of ballads, some of which he wrote himself, and died in 1758.

That the Clearances started when they did in the latter half of the eighteenth century was probably inevitable: the sober fact is that they made sound commercial sense. England was going through a period of peace and economic well-being which it was willing to share with its poorer neighbour to the north. But the Scots are a stubborn people, and a loyal one – southerners and borderers might submit, or at least agree to co-operate; the Highlanders did not. The accession of James the First – or Sixth – to the joint throne might have been expected to bring about a rapprochement; so might Queen Anne's Treaty of Union of 1707. What in fact happened was a widening of the gap between the Scots in the south who looked to England and the Highlands and Islands. 'To the southern inhabitants of Scotland, the state of the mountains and the islands is equally unknown with that of Borneo and Sumatra. Of both they have only heard a little, and guess the rest. They are strangers to the language and manners, to the advantages and wants of the people, whose life they would model, and whose evils they would remedy', said Dr Johnson. But he was quick to see that with the weakening of their chiefs, the whole economic structure of the Islands was already doomed. Johnson apprehended what the author of 'English Social History', G. M. Trevelyan, was to say, 'The whole manner of life and society, which had prevailed in the mountains of Scotland with little change since prehistoric times, was swept away at a blow. The tribal system, the kilted warrior with broadsword and target (*sic*), the patriarchal chief vanished for ever.'

After the Risings, when England was determined to put all resistance down, Redcoats scouring the moors for Jacobites on the run were assisted by newly recruited Scottish regiments, among them, the Black Watch (so named because its tartan of black and green is among the darkest) raised in 1729. To do them justice, the Highlanders and Islanders were no mere rebels – the word Rebellion in connection with the Risings is not used in Northern Scotland. Their long history had taught them to regard the Stuarts – kings descended from Robert the Bruce – as their national and proper rulers; the Hanovers, as usurpers. The Georges had in fact done rather well by their new country, but the Highlands wanted no part in England's growing affluence. Highland opposition was further stiffened by the memory of ancient clan feuds. And on Mull, Argyll and his Campbells who sided with the new regime, were the traditional enemy. Macleans were not ready to forgive their powerful neighbour, any more than MacDonalds could forget Glencoe. But the centre of power was inexorably moving south. The Borders and southern Scotland had profited greatly from the relaxation of trade barriers, and Glasgow, in particular, had been quick to take advantage of the new opportunities offered to its merchants. Walter Scott's Bailie Nicol Jarvie was well aware of this. A well-known scene in 'Rob Roy' has him entertaining friends to an after-dinner bowl of brandy punch, to which he proudly adds fresh limes imported from the West Indies – a novelty now readily available. The conversation is all of trade, and the benefits it has brought to the whole region. The good Bailie is loud in his praise of local products: 'We hae our Stirling serge, Musselburgh stuffs, Aberdeen hose, Edinburgh shalloons, and the like for our woollen and worsted goods – and we hae linens of a'kinds too and cheaper than you hae in Lunnon itsel' – and we can buy your north o'England wares, as Manchester wares, Sheffield wares, and Newcastle earthenware, as cheap as you can at Liverpool.' Such luxuries and the growth in the money supply which made their purchase possible meant nothing to the crofters of the north. Living self-sufficient in a remote, enclosed community, they seldom handled money – most of their rents they paid in kind, built their own houses and provided their own food and clothing. Practically their only contact with the outside world of commerce came through the cattle markets. The small black cattle that the drovers herded down to the shore along well-marked tracks still visible (and walkable) across the moor had little in common with the splendid beasts bred on Mull nowadays on which thousands of cameras are trained during the tourist season. 'Black Cattle' are now a registered rare breed; the cows grazing quietly on the hill-side, their shaggy coats the colour of marma-lade, with soft eyes under the wide span of their long horns, are very different from the small animals which arrived to be sold on the hoof at the fairs of Forfar and Crieff. They were probably half starved and certainly exhausted after being driven a hundred miles and more. They had been fed on a meagre diet of moor grass and when winter came, bedded down on poor straw or bracken. Before the introduction of the rotation of crops, which was being pioneered in England, there was next to no winter fodder. The horrid practice of 'bleeding' – drawing fresh blood from the stabled animals to enrich the crofters' poor ration of porridge – would have weakened them further. Then, cattle from the Western Isles had to be rowed or swum across, before setting off on their journey to the mainland markets. They were tied horn to tail, but in rough weather, the line sometimes broke, as James Hogg, known to literature as the 'Ettrick Shepherd', discovered during a journey which took him to Mull. In a letter to his patron, Walter Scott, he describes the scene: 'To the westward (of Jura) about half a mile, we first saw a large wherry crouding sail to the South, and then, a good way ahead of her, a black thing came on with the tide, which we soon discovered, with the help of the spyglass, to be an excellent black highland cow. We approached quite near them, and saw them overtake her, when they immediately dropped their sail and threw coils of ropes around her, endeavouring with all their might to haul her into the boat: this however they were unable to effect, for she splashed like a whale; and the boat was like to turn its keel uppermost; but they lashed her to the stern.' Within moments a second half-drowned animal appeared, 'a dun cow emerged from below the waves about forty yards to the N.W. of us. She was grown very weak, was swimming with her side uppermost, and blowing like a porpoise; but the tide bare her rapidly away from us, and very near straight for them . . . they at last with some difficulty succeeded in securing that also, when they made slowly toward the land.' The letter was written from Tobermory in 1804, a half-way stage in the journey which James Hogg, with his friend William Laidlaw, was making to Harris where he intended to buy a sheep run, with the £200 he had saved from the publication of his works. The Border shepherd turned poet failed in his attempt to turn sheep farmer, but his letters were serialised in various literary magazines and they provide a very vivid picture of the Western Isles during the Clearances.

All might have been well if it had been only the new breeds – hardy Cheviots and black-face – which had been brought in, but they arrived from the Borders and the north of England along with their shepherds and flock-masters. Sheep had always been bred in the islands, valued chiefly for their fleece which kept the crofters in their homespun clothing. The ewe's milk made cheese, and the animals were seldom slaughtered as little meat was eaten. There had been no sheep farming on a large scale, though it was particularly well suited to moorland, and very profitable. But the benefits by-passed the crofters for there were by now few landlords, themselves hard pressed for cash, who could afford to turn down the large sums they were offered to disappropriate their tenants. With the evictions, the last links were broken between the chiefs and their clansmen. The ruins of abandoned townships and deserted villages are tangible evidence of the damage done – Gribun, a little to the north of the west coast cliff line has no more than half a dozen houses; all the homesteads in the locality known as Sorne were burnt down to make room for the fine house built in 1860 on the Glengorm estate; along the shores of Lake Tuath, villages are buried in bracken, others, south of Dervaig near Glenbellart stand empty. Schoolhouses no longer needed are left isolated and roofless chapels are left to crumble back into the moor. Crofting of course continues, notably on the fine private estates in the district of Bunessan, a pleasant modernised village half-way down the Ross of Mull, and in a new development, many of the unroofed croft houses are being bought, restored and fitted up as so-called holiday homes.

These houses, from the late eighteenth or early nineteenth centuries, are not 'black houses', a term which puzzles new arrivals in the Hebrides, where the stone walls of cottages are either whitewashed or left in their natural state. Black houses go back to the days before chimneys when the peat fire was lit in the middle of the main room, and its smoke drifting up encrusted the rafters and upper walls till they took on a deep, dark varnish which recalls the paintings of the old Dutch masters. 'Black houses' along with the 'mud huts' remarked on by travellers, gave way to bigger dwellings, first thatched and later, roofed with slate. The method of construction was similar – a 'roof tree' from which coupled timbers depended was supported by the gable ends of the dry-stone walls. The timbers were then covered with carefully tailored divots and the thatch placed on. The first chimneys were in the gable ends – in Mull, some cottages kept one rounded end, while the other was squared off to accommodate the chimney. By the middle of the eighteenth century the croft houses became larger, consisting of a living room,

with an adjoining sleeping room, as well as a separate cow byre. The chimney now appeared in the middle of the roof; sometimes, there were two chimneys, one at each end. These dwellings were surprisingly warm for the walls were very thick – up to six foot in the Outer Isles. Peat being plentiful, the fire was kept going day in day out, covered over or 'smoored' at night to keep the heat in the smouldering peats. But with their earthen floors, they were damp, and in rough weather the rain dripped through the thatch, which needed replacing at least every two years.

The construction of his house was the crofter's first task, and with the whole village helping in days when most of the work was done in common, it went up very quickly. The most valuable part was the roof timber – the fact that it was often fashioned from driftwood from shipwrecks suggests that wood was already growing scarce. The crofter regarded the roof tree as his private property and, if he removed, took it with him. This was one of the Highlanders' many rights, endorsed by tradition perhaps rather than by law, which are summed up by an old Gaelic proverb:

'A wand from the wood, taken at will,
A fish from the stream, a deer from the
    hill;
Why grows this gap 'twixt Cot and Hall?
These three are rights God gave to all.'

It is quoted by the poet, Alastair Maclean, in his book on Ardnamurchan, the bleak peninsula that juts out north of Morvern. It reflects the rather cavalier attitude taken towards game laws – as Mull sees it, it was not the landowner who put the trout in the stream and the deer on the hill.

It was towards the end of the Clearances that Glengorm House went up, and the local historian of Mull, Peter MacNab, tells how the district came to change its name. Glengorm, meaning the 'blue glen' was suggested to the English-speaking landlord, who having no Gaelic missed the covert reference to the colour of the smoke which rose from the homesteads burnt down to make way for his estate. At about the same time, Ulva was being cleared – in 1840, the island supported a population of about eight hundred; ten years later, only two hundred were left. In the vicinity, Calgary Bay is one of the last – and most famous – landmarks associated with the sorry history of enforced emigration. At the height of the season, the long beach of immaculate shell sand, with bold cliffs as outposts and as backdrop, a sweep of the sea-grass the Hebrides call 'machair' reaching up to wooded hills, is inundated with tourists who may or may not remember that in 1883 ships were calling to transfer dispossessed crofters on their way to Canada. Whether they founded and christened the city of Calgary is now in dispute. The Clearances came to an end, but two World Wars and the ravages of over-cropping have reduced the population of Mull by an estimated 85 per cent. Most of the present inhabitants live in the northern half of

Dervaig

the island – in Salen, and Tobermory, and
Dervaig. In Mull, as elsewhere in the Highlands and Islands, there are endless places that
recall the evictions, but I sometimes think
that the silence of Glenmore is their most
poignant momento, for there the solitude is
man-made. At the entrance to the Glen, Loch
Don, the 'brown' loch so-called after the long
mudflats exposed when the tide is out, was
once a busy landing stage. It is the shortest
crossing point from Oban and the mainland
and was used by cattle drovers as well as occasional travellers. James Hogg called there:
'As we dreaded again to encounter the tides in
the sound of Mull we came to anchor in Loch
Don.' Then, with a companion, he 'went and
spent the evening at the house of Auchnacraig
in Mull, which is a good inn and kept by civil
people'. The Drovers Inn is still there on
Grass Point, but along the once busy shores
of Loch Don, there remains only a straggling
hamlet, a fit introduction to the wastes of the

glen. The moor is empty, stretching out to the heights where small herds of deer can be glimpsed along the skyline. I have heard it said that there are twice as many deer on Mull as people. Here and there, empty croft houses are up for sale; there are practically no sheep. The sky is reflected in lonely lochans – on one of them is a fortified islet, ringed with a stone wall at water level – which in ancient times served as a safe haven from marauders and other foes. In spring, the moor is delightful with wild flowers – bluebells and cotton grass unfolding its puffballs, and by the water's edge, platoons of wild iris standing to attention under their gold helmets. During the winter months, the glen lies quiet under the snow and high in the February sky, eagles perform the aerobatics of their courtship. With the return of warm weather, tourists come back in their coaches travelling much the same road that the pilgrims, assembled at Grass Point, once took to Fionnphort and the Sacred Isle of Iona.

V

The Island

Iona has many names – Hii, Hy, I, Ia, Io, Y, Yi are the ones Neil Gunn selected for a chapter heading in 'Off in a Boat.' 'I', pronounced like the letter 'e' in English, is simply the Gaelic word for an island; this island indissolubly linked with St Columba became better known as Icolmkill, or the 'island of the cell (or church) of Columba,' though spellings vary widely. Martin, who used this name, explains its origins as follows: 'This Isle in the Irish language is called I. Colmkil, i.e. the Isthmus of Columbus the Clergy-Man. Colum was his proper name, and the Addition of Kil, which signifies a Church, was added by the Islanders by way of excellence; for there were few Churches then in the remote and lesser Isles.' Martin also gives another reason for calling Iona, I. 'The Natives have a Tradition among them, that one of the Clergy-Men who accompanied Columbus in his voyage thither, having at a good distance espied the Isle, and cry'd joyfully to Columbus in the Irish language, Chi Mi, i.e. I see her; meaning thereby the Country of which they had been in quest; that Columbus then answered, It shall be from henceforth called Y.'

Icolmkill, however, gained the edge – Shakespeare refers to it, and to its famous burial ground, in Macbeth. Two noblemen, discussing the murder of King Duncan, a killing which brings Macbeth to the throne, ask: 'Where is Duncan's body?' The answer:

'Carried to Colme-kill,
The sacred store-house of his predecessors
And guardian of their bones.'

A stubborn belief persists that Macbeth in turn was buried there. The success of Columba's mission turned the little island of Iona which he made his headquarters into one of the holy places of the western hemisphere, and as such a fit sepulchre of kings. Dr Johnson called it, 'that illustrious Island, which was once the luminary of the Caledonian regions, where savage clans and roving bar-

barians derived the benefits of knowledge, and the blessings of religion.' In one of his most often quoted pronouncements, he added: 'That man is little to be envied, whose patriotism would not gain Force upon the plain of Marathon, or whose piety would not grow warmer among the ruins of Iona!'

For fourteen hundred years, pilgrims have been coming to Iona in search of sanctification, but even the merely curious have shown a spirit of reverence. In later years, Bowman said much the same as Johnson: 'It is ... not easy for a philosophic mind to approach (Iona's) shores and tread the royal and pious dust which it contains, without feeling the influence of the recollections they are calcu-

Iona Abbey
and St Oran's Chapel

lated to excite. He who can here abstract himself from the living objects around him, and abandon his mind to the vision of the past, will long after recur, with feelings of pleasing melancholy, to the short time he has spent among the tombs of Iona.' Perhaps the most telling tribute to the spirit of Iona was paid by the King of Norway, Magnus Barelegs, when he visited it in 1097. He was on his way to plunder Islay, but according to the sagas, spared Iona where, 'he gave peace and quarter to all men, and to the households of all men'. By then Columba had been dead five hundred years, during which his renown had spread throughout Western Europe bringing fame to the tiny territory from which he operated.

Iona is no more than three miles long and about one mile across. Its only natural landmark is the hill of Dun I which rises to over 300 feet. It is a beautiful island, but very different from Mull. Though only a mile separates them, Iona seems rather to belong to the Outer Hebrides where the Atlantic holds sway. Like them, it is virtually barren of trees and its coasts are edged by fine white sands backed by machair. The best beaches are in the north, and on the west coast where Port Ban stands at the head of a long shallow bay, shaped like the new moon, which has the fairy-story name of 'The Bay at the Back of the Ocean'. Further down, the south-west corner, where great waves break on the sea-cliffs, is open to the full force of the Atlantic weather. Bowman, who knew Iona as Strona, the 'Isle of Billows' experienced something of this as he crossed the rough twelve miles from Staffa to land on a rocky beach hereabouts. 'Here', he wrote, 'the vast Atlantic ocean bears on it with all its force, and no land to the westward is seen to streak or stud the interminable expanse of the waters.'

Nowadays, as in the old days when pilgrims crowded to Iona, the usual approach is by Fionnphort where a ferry crosses the sound continuously. In the season, it is sometimes possible to make the whole journey by sea from Oban. Other travellers, however, have preferred the Bull's Hole as a starting place. A short distance up the coast from Fionnphort, it is sheltered by the Isle of Women and is generally thought to provide good anchorage. Thomas Pennant, whom Dr Johnson considered the best travel writer of the day, thought it the safest. The success of his 'Tour of Scotland' which came out in 1769 encouraged him to make a second journey three years later. The journals he kept became the 'Voyage to the Hebrides'. Pennant started from Helensburgh where he boarded the cutter, Lady Frederick Campbell. Coming from the south, he approached Iona from Jura, spending an anxious night hove to near the 'tremendous chain' of the Torran Rocks. The next morning found the ship at anchor in the Sound of Iona, 'in three fathoms of water, on a white sandy bottom'. But the best anchorage in Pennant's view was the Bull Hole, 'on the East side, between a little island and that of Mull. This sound is three miles long and

one broad, shallow, and in some parts dry at
the ebb of spring tides: it is bounded on the
East by the Island of Mull, on the West, by
that of Iona, the most celebrated of the
Hebrides.' He was amused by the activity of
multitudes of gannets, which 'precipitated
themselves from a vast height, plunged on
their prey at least two fathoms deep, and took
to the air again as soon as they emerged'. He
went on to give his first impressions of Iona:
'The view of Iona is very picturesque: the
East side, or that which bounds the sound,
exhibited a beautiful variety; an extent of
plain, a little elevated above the water, and
almost covered with the ruins of the sacred
buildings, and with the remains of the old
town still inhabited. Beyond these the island
rises into little rocky hills, with narrow verdant hollows between (for they merit not the
name of vallies) and numerous enough for
every recluse to take his solitary walk, undis-
turbed by society.'

Pennant landed on Iona at the Bay of Martyrs, just south of St Ronan's Bay, and
encamped there on the moor. Incidentally,
Pennant believed that the spot where he dis-
embarked was 'the place where the bodies of
those who were to be interred in holy ground
were received, during the period of superstition'. It may have been, for the bodies of
the great intended for burial on Iona were
transported long distances, the cortege often
resting at night on small islands in the lochs,
where they were safe from the depredations
of wolves or raiders. But the Bay of Martyrs

is now remembered as the site of a massacre of the monks by Norse invaders early in the eighth century. There are other similar sites on the island, notably Traigh Ban, the White Strand of the Monks, very near the top of the east coast, where raiding Norsemen arrived in the year 986.

After visiting the abbey and the ancient monuments surrounding it, which he catalogued carefully, Pennant went to see another famous landmark associated with St Columba. 'Cross the island over a most fertile elevated tract to the S. West side, to visit the landing place of St Columba: a small bay with a pebbly beach, mixed with a variety of pretty stones.... On one side is shewn an oblong heap of earth, the supposed size of the vessel that transported St Columba and his twelve disciples from Ireland to this island.' On modern maps the spot appears as Port a' Churaich, the Harbour of the Coracle, and the mound supposedly covering the vessel is still there. According to a persistent tradition, it was buried out of sight lest Columba should be tempted to return to Ireland. The pretty story of St Columba and the crane reflects the theme of his home-sickness: the weather-beaten bird, blown off course, was found on the shore, and by Columba's orders, was tended by the monks till it was fit to fly back to Ireland, its home – and Columba's. 'For when (the crane's) three days housing was ended, and as her host stood by, she rose in first flight from the earth into high heaven, and after a while at gaze to spy out

her aerial way, took her straight flight above the quiet sea, and so to Ireland through the tranquil weather.' Thus the story ends, as translated by Helen Waddell from a 'Life of St Columbus' written early in the eleventh century.

In the fourteen hundred years and more since the Irish princeling Columba set out on his mission, historians and hagiographers have been fighting it out. And in a country where the bardic tradition is strong, facts grow hard to establish where legend takes over. For Columba's arrival on Iona, however, we have a date, a very precise one – the 12th of May 563. And for the boat in which

he sailed, a detailed description which fits
in closely with what is known of the vessels
of the day. As Martin was told, 'Columbus's
Boat called Curich ... was made of Ribs
of Wood, and the Outside cover'd with
Hides; the Boat was long, and sharp-pointed
at both ends.' Martin also mentions 'the dock'
which was dug out on the shore to preserve
it. One version of Columba's journey from
Ireland has him landing first in the Garvellach
islands, the 'Isles of the Sea' at the mouth of
the Firth in Lorn. Sometimes he is accompanied by eleven followers; sometimes by
twelve. It is believed that his mother, Eithne,
lies buried there. Whether Columba ever

intended to settle in the Garvellachs can only be surmised; the most popular reason given for his moving further on is that these islands are within sight of Ireland whereas Iona is not. Eithne's reputed resting-place is on the southernmost island of the group: Eileach nam Naoimh, the island of the Saint. On the northernmost, there stood the formidable stronghold of Dunconnel, seat of Conal, king of Dalriada, ruler of the Pictish territory which Columba was about to conquer for Christianity. The two men were related, and it was Conal who granted Columba the lands of Iona. When Conal died in 574, it was Columba who inaugurated Aidan, the cousin who succeeded him, the ceremony taking place in the monastery on Iona.

The ancient kingdom of Dalriada was set up in the fifth century when the Irish took advantage of the vacuum left by the Romans' withdrawal from Britain to invade. The lands they eventually held, including the Western Islands, covered about a fourth of the Hibernian peninsula; in course of time, they gave their name, Scotii or Scots, to the whole country. Of the people they conquered, the Picts, who had been there for a thousand years and more, very little is known for certain. 'The painted people' as some still call them are thought to have come from Central Europe, from the region of the Black Sea, in one of the great tribal movements which preceded the Christian era; the language they spoke was a form of Celtic; their religion, part of the Druidic cult. Their territory stretched from Caithness in the north to the Forth in the south, taking in the Hebrides. Christianity had not reached them, for although it had penetrated as far as Strathclyde where St Ninian had established his great monastery at Wigtown (Candida Casa) at the end of the fourth century, it had made little impact further north. Nor had Columba's predecessors from Ireland – St Oran, for instance, who founded religious settlements on Iona itself, as well as on Mull and Tiree, and died of a plague in 548, or St Brendan of Clonfert who erected a chapel and built beehive cells for his monks in the Garvellachs in 542. Another near contemporary, St Moluag, settled with his monks on the island of Lismore. It was left to Columba to complete and consolidate their work during a mission which was political as well as religious. When he died in 597 the Picts were both Christianised and subdued and the kings of Dalriada safe on their throne – till the end of the 9th century when the west coast and the islands fell to the Norsemen.

A great deal has been written about Columba, much of it quite soon after his death. He was praised by Bede, the great ecclesiastical scholar who spanned the seventh and eighth centuries; a very early 'Life' was compiled by Adamnan, who became Abbot of Iona in 679. Adamnan was able to talk to several of Columba's monks, and may have had access to some of his writings which were subsequently dispersed and lost without trace during the Norse raids. But his is a work of reverence rather than history, and he gives us few hard facts.

We know that Columba was born at Gartan, in Co. Donegal, somewhere between 518 and 523, of noble parentage. He was intended for the Church and became the pupil of the famous Irish bishop, St Finnian. After being ordained, he founded the church of Derry and the monastery of Durrow. Later he is said to have founded a number of churches in Scotland, but information is scarce and patchy. Columba was in his early forties when he set out from Ireland, possibly under a cloud: from a very early period, it was commonly believed that he had been sent into exile as a penance for having fomented clan rivalries and taken part in the bloody skirmishes that resulted. There are certainly many contemporary reports of his quick and most unChristian-like temper. Of his travels in Scotland, there are few details and many of the sites associated with him – his landing place on Skye, for instance – cannot be authenticated. In some ways, Columba remains a legendary figure, never more so than in his encounter with the Loch Ness monster. As Adamnan tells it, Columba was on his way to Inverness when he encountered a group of mourners lamenting the death of a local man seized by the monster. Nevertheless, Columba ordered one of his followers to swim the river to collect a boat from the further shore so that his party could cross in comfort. The monster appeared but as it was about to grab the terrified swimmer, Columba, making the sign of the cross, forbade it to approach and it 'fled more quickly than if it had been pulled back by ropes'. In a similar way, by invoking the name of God in fervent prayer, he destroyed a wild boar on Skye. The appeal of such stories in a credulous age is evident, and they are meat and drink to Adamnan whose work consists largely of instances of heavenly visions, prophecies and miraculous happenings – how Columba cured the sick, mending broken bones and healing deadly diseases, how he improved both cattle and crops, turning bitter fruit into sweet, bringing on the harvest, and of how he drew water from hard rock by the power of prayer. He predicted the presence of salmon, calmed tempests and drove a demon out of a milk pail. Occasionally he took revenge on those who had displeased him. Angels and whales, weird sea creatures and wild animals make their appearance in Adamnan's pages and we are told why there are no snakes on Iona. The exiling of snakes (and some say, frogs) was one of the Saint's last miracles.

'On a certain day in that same summer in which he passed to the Lord, the saint went in a chariot to visit some of the brethren, who were engaged in some heavy work in the western part of the Ionan island.' After telling them that his death was near, 'the saint tried to comfort them as best he could; and, raising both his holy hands, he blessed the whole of this our island, saying: "From this very moment poisonous reptiles shall in no way be able to hunt men or cattle in this island, so long as the inhabitants shall continue to observe the commandments of Christ."'' As anglers know all too well, the ban does not extend to Mull. However, there are no adders on Coll or Tiree. Adamnan's account of Columba's death includes another popular medieval legend: an old white packhorse who served to carry the monastery's milk pails came up to the saint as he was resting on the moor. 'Strange to say, (it) laid its head on his bosom, and knowing that its master was about to leave it, and that it would see him no more – began to utter plaintive cries, and like a human being, to shed copious tears on the saint's bosom, foaming and greatly wailing.' The date generally accepted for Columba's death is 597 – he died quietly at the foot of the altar between the 8th and 9th of June, comforted by the angels which figured so largely in his life.

Tourists are still shown the Angels' Knoll (also known as Sithean Mor or the Great Fairies Mound) where Columba was observed at prayer by a prying monk who saw white-robed angels fluttering round him. They will also see his cell, Tor Abb, now a grass grown hillock opposite the Abbey, and the height on the moor known as the Hill with its Back to Ireland, which Columba climbed to make sure that the country of his birth was well and truly out of sight. But most of the landmarks he would have recognised have long since disappeared, including the Black Stone, a great block of basalt, on which the most solemn oaths were sworn, and the three hundred and sixty sculptured crosses, probably dating back to Druidic times, which were condemned in 1560 as 'monuments of idolatrie' by the Synod of Argyll which ordered them to be thrown into the sea. The early Celtic church was more tolerant, allowing ancient beliefs and practices to co-exist comfortably with Christianity. It is no surprise that the Angels' Knoll should also be the Fairies's Hill, nor that the Spouting Cave, further down the west coast, remained dedicated to that dangerous sea god, Shonny, who could be propitiated by regular offerings of porridge, and mead, and ale thrown from the cave's mouth. Shonny has remained Shonny, tamed in local nursery rhymes; he was superseded by St Michael, the victorious, patron saint of seafarers as well as horsemen. The festival of Michaelmas was once the greatest in the Christian calendar, but the Michaelmas cavalcade and other celebrations have borrowed much from ancient pagan rites.

As to the Abbey itself, only its emplacement dates back to Columba's times. First seen from Fionnphort, standing stark and solid between the empty moor and the sky, it bears no relation to the group of cells constructed of daub and wattle and the primitive chapel which made up the original foundation. For protection, these were surrounded by a ditch and ramparts of which traces are still visible. The Abbey as we now see it is the result of dedicated work by the Iona Community, a body of laymen gathered together before the Second World War by the once fashionable Edinburgh preacher, The Reverend George Macleod, to restore Iona's sacred monuments. The first Abbey was built towards the end of the thirteenth century on the orders of Reginald, son of Somerled, Lord of the Isles. The building it replaced had long since decayed: the final Norse raid in 986, during which Columba's shrine was desecrated, had left very little above ground level. And when the Benedictines arrived, the Celtic Church itself had fallen into disfavour. Though it owed obedience to the Church of Rome, it had developed along its own lines, especially where the ritual was concerned. The shape of a monk's tonsure or the date of Easter may seem small matters, but of such schisms were born, and from the time of King David, the Scottish Crown was determined to bring the Church of the Culdees (as it was now called) into line. After the Norman Conquest, Malcolm Canmore's English Queen, St Margaret, contributed to the rebuilding of what was now the Abbey of Iona and was canonised in 1151 for her benefactions to the Church. After the Reformation, disrepair set in again – in his day, Pennant reported that many of the monastic buildings were being used as byres.

The restoration work undertaken by the Iona Community has been most faithful and the general effect is much as it must have been in the thirteenth century, but only the learned in ecclesiastical architecture can hope to disentangle the dates of the various parts of the present complex. Of more immediate appeal are St Oran's Chapel and the three Crosses opposite the West Door of the Abbey. Of these, St John's is a modern replica of the eighth century original; only the truncated shaft of St Matthew's remains. But St Martin's Cross, also of the eighth century, stands erect, a solid block, magnificently carved from the stone called epediorite. It is a splendid example of two cultures blending – one face covered with ornamental designs of Pictish origin, the other with biblical scenes, David playing the harp, Daniel in the lions' den, around the central Virgin and Child.

St Oran's Chapel, restored this century, dates back to the twelfth century – a simple, rectangular Norman building with a triple row of chevron decoration in its fine arched door. It presides over the famous burial ground of the kings – Reilig Oran. Dean Munro, who visited Iona in 1594, found Latin inscriptions indicating the tombs of forty-eight Scottish, Irish and Norwegian kings. There was also talk of a French king, though I have never seen him named. The inscriptions have vanished; once there was a 'ridge' of captains and a 'ridge' of kings, but 'slight remains' were all that Pennant could find and the modern tourist can hardly hope to do better. Reilig Oran is a place in which to recollect rather than to observe, and perhaps to remember the curious legend woven round the original Oran. Columba received a heavenly intimation that the chapel could never be completed without a human sacrifice. So one of the oldest monks, Oran, volunteered

to be immolated. A few days after he had
been buried alive, Columba had the grave
opened only to hear Oran, still living, or
perhaps returned from the dead, say: 'There is
no such great wonder in death, nor is hell
what it has been described.' Such blasphemy
earned Oran a prompt reburial. Though there
is no documentary evidence for the tale, it is
firmly embedded in popular lore and must
surely be considered another instance of
the merging of Druidic practice with
Christianity.

Easier to find than the graves of Reilig
Oran is the processional way leading from the
shore through the village to the Abbey. With

The Nunnery

its paving carefully restored, it is known as
the Street of the Dead. It leads past two other
of Iona's finest monuments, Maclean's Cross
and the Nunnery. The Cross, which dates
from the fifteenth century, shows a crucifix-
ion on one face while the other is covered
with Pictish decorative designs. It stands outside the Nunnery, which was founded by the
Benedictines along with the Abbey – Reginald's sister became its first abbess. The
remains are substantial, a tall and stately
group of buildings, round carefully mown
lawns where the nuns once went silently to
prayer or took their simple recreation. There
are deep borders of the valerian – pink and

Maclean's Cross

white and crimson – which has rooted itself in the old walls. The Nunnery has been described as one of the most beautiful of Scotland's ancient monuments. But Columba would not have approved, since he is said to have exiled all womenfolk to Eilean nam Ban, the islet at the entrance to the Bull Hole. According to tradition, their cows went with them in accordance with the proverb that says, in its English version:

'Where there is a cow,
There will be a woman;
And where there is a woman,
There will be mischief.'

It is hardly likely that the ban could have applied to all Iona's womenfolk: it seems more probable that only those working directly for the monastery were found quarters at a distance. Whatever the practice may have been, women have had their revenge in the cult of St Bride. A local girl, a simple shepherdess, she was transported by angels to Bethlehem on the first Christmas Eve to help tend the infant Jesus whom she wrapped in her plaid. Whether or not this St Bride is the Brigit of Druidic times, the illegitimate daughter of an Irish prince shipwrecked on Iona where she was held in high esteem as a sacred Virgin, the two are indissolubly locked in legend. Just as St Columba has his flower, St John's Wort, St Bride has her bird – the elegant oyster-catcher that paces along the shore in his orange gaiters and matching beak.

VI
Days at Sea

As the ferry from Fionnphort chugs off to
Iona, another boat sails out on the longer,
twelve-mile journey to Staffa, crowded with
passengers eager to see, and if possible to
explore, Fingal's Cave. This remarkable
natural phenomenon makes the small island
off the West coast of Mull one of the most
visited in the Hebrides. It is due to the nature
of the soil, pure basalt practically black in
tone, which when exposed to the weather
tends to split lengthwise into hexagonal columns. Staffa was obviously known to the
Vikings, who named it Stave Island, after the
wooden shafts which supported their houses.
But it was not 'discovered' until 1772, and
then only by accident, when the naturalist and
explorer, Joseph Banks, stopped off on Mull
on his way to Iceland. While staying with one
of the Macleans, he met an Englishman, a Mr
Leach, who told him of an extraordinary
island 'nine leagues off' whose columns of
basalt surpassed Ireland's famous Giant's
Causeway. The island was too small to
provide harbour for the ship on which Banks
and his party were travelling to the Arctic, so
a yawl was hired and they set off from Tobermory. The wind had dropped and the passage
was slow, but the crew was able to row them
in safety to Staffa. Night had fallen and it was
too dark to do any exploring, so they set up

camp and started off at day-break for the cave. Banks, who described it as 'one of the greatest natural curiosities in the world' took measurements – the ranges of pillars standing in colonnades were about 55 feet high and nearly 5 feet in diameter; the cave's overall length being 371 feet, it was 115 feet high and 51 feet wide. Sketches were made, and subsequently engraved, by the artist who accompanied Banks, John Cleveley Jnr.

Banks asked his guide what the cave was called and was told it was known as Fhinn, or Fingal's Cave, but how or when it was given this name is not clear. There is no question, however, that its association with the legendary Irish hero, an account of whose deeds had been published in MacPherson's Ossianic cycle, stimulated curiosity and earned it much publicity. 'Fingal, an ancient epic poem in six books' appeared in 1762; its author, a penniless young Scottish poet, James MacPherson (1736–1796) asserted that the works were translated from the Gaelic of Ossian, a notable third century bard. Ossian was the

97

son of Fhinn MacConal, righter of wrongs and defender of the oppressed; as a young man he had been seduced by a fairy princess and had spent three days with her in Tir-nan-og, the land of the ever-young beyond the western seas, before returning to earth. The three days turned out to have been three centuries and Ossian found that his father's deeds had been forgotten. Now an old man, with flowing white locks and some say blind, he spent the rest of his days travelling the country with his harp celebrating Fingal at fireside gatherings. Coming as it did as the Age of Reason was beginning to give way to a Romantic revival, MacPherson's book became a runaway best-seller, translated into all the main European languages. But there were those, Dr Johnson among them, who suspected a forgery. And a committee appointed after MacPherson's death to investigate the poem's origins found that most of them had been composed by the author himself. Nevertheless, Dr Johnson was ready enough to see the island 'so lately raised to renown by Mr. Banks', but he shared the experience of so many latter day tourists and was unable to land. Boswell, who was with him, wrote: 'We saw the island of Staffa at no great distance, but could not land upon it, the surge was so high on its rocky coast.' Pennant, too was unlucky – sailing from Iona, a fresh south-westerly churned up a heavy sea and made a landing impossible. Bowman and his party had better luck – though there was a heavy swell, the sea was as smooth as glass as their ship sailed between the Treshnish Islands and the coast.

'The shores of Mull on the eastward lay,
And Ulva dark and Colonsay
And all the group of islands gay
That guard fam'd Staffa round.'

They dropped anchor in the south-eastern corner of the island which 'appeared like a huge ark floating on the sea, the sides, as it were, composed of multitudes of straight, angular shafts or narrow pilasters clustered together, and covered with an irregular thick stratum of alluvium, which gives it a heavy appearance. It is so totally different from every other object in nature, that it is difficult not to believe it a work of art, though its magnitude at once repressed that idea.'

The weather still holding, the company boarded two rowing boats and was able to enter Fingal's cave 'riding on the breakers'; its appearance, later written up in his journal, reminded Bowman, as it did Mendelssohn, of a Gothic minster, 'the sides being perfectly columnar and clustered, some in projecting groups and others as pilasters on spacious walls, the roof fretted and studded with thousands of polygonal sections, like corbels, groins, and armorial escutcheons, the bases resting on or having before them, others, broken off at all heights, as though they were stalls, niches and steps'. There are other caves on Staffa, and Bowman explored them all – the Great Cave, the Boat Cave, the Cormorant's, the Clamshell or Scallop-shell

Cave. Before leaving for Iona, he took copious notes, completed a sketch and paced the Great Causeway.

Though the legendary origin of the Fingal epic had been disproved, his Cave remained the cynosure of the Romantics, a must in their itinerary of the Highlands and Islands. Turner painted it, poets visited it, including Wordsworth and Keats; in the summer of 1810, Sir Walter Scott made it a port of call. But Staffa is probably most often thought of in conjunction with Mendelssohn's 'Hebridean Overture', commonly known as Fingal's Cave, which the composer called 'that cathedral of the sea'. Bowman, however, notes that an older name was Uaimh Binn, meaning the musical cave, and the overture has naturally enough been associated with the surge and swell of the sea, and the roar of the great rollers breaking on the cliffs. According to a less romantic version of how it came to be written, another kind of pounding is said to have inspired it. Mendelssohn was a poor sailor and as soon as he had embarked for Staffa, took to his cabin, where he lay in distress throughout the trip. Suffering from nausea and a severe headache, his condition was not improved by the relentless hammering of the steam engine which came through the cabin wall.

The rich tapestry of islands spread out before Mull's west coast is best left to yachtsmen, though passengers on cruises soon learn to identify them. Some are no more than skerries and rocky reefs, others are topped with green moorlands which provided extra pasture for the black cattle and sheep which were ferried over. Most are now uninhabited. From a long list of magical names, the Treshnish Isles, eight in all, stretching out over four miles, are best known for the Dutchman's Cap, whose outline soon becomes familiar. In early times, the northernmost isle (Cairnburg Mor) harboured a garrison which was perpetually on the look-out for Viking raids. On Lunga, auks build their nests, and during the mating season in the autumn, grey seals make it their breeding ground. Even when landing is impossible, a day spent cruising is worthwhile for the sight of the sea-birds – some local, auks and puffins, shags, petrels, kittiwakes; others in transit, like the many kinds of geese and the whooper swans flying south for the winter. It is these birds in their thousands that fertilise with their droppings the grass which seems to grow straight out of barren rock.

It was from Inch Kenneth that Johnson and Boswell attempted Staffa and having failed to land made up for their disappointment by visiting MacKinnon's Cave near at hand on Mull. In a 'strong good boat, with four stout rowers' they followed the coast till they reached Gribun where they found the cave 'in a rock of great height close to the sea'. The cave itself, Boswell says, seemed to be very lofty, and to be 'a pretty regular arch'. Having forgotten to provide themselves with tapers, they explored by candlelight, penetrating very deep, 'no less than four-hundred-and-eight-five feet'. Johnson confirms all this, adding: 'the place well repaid our trouble'. Both their journals record something of the legends attached to the cave: in some detail Johnson describes how they found a second cave within which stood 'a square stone called, as we are told, Fingal's Table'. Johnson also mentions former explorers, 'some who are reported never to have returned'; Boswell elaborates: 'Tradition says that a piper and twelve men advanced into this cave, nobody can tell how far; and never returned.' MacKinnon's Cave certainly has an evil reputation with stories of fairies who lure those who enter it to their death. Sinister tales are attached to other caves, notably on Skye, which involve a piper, sometimes accompanied by his dog who can still be heard barking all the way from fairyland. As most of the caves in the Hebrides are tidal, it seems more than likely that the unwary should have been engulfed and drowned as the sea rushes in.

During their expedition to MacKinnon's Cave, Johnson and Boswell were able to admire some fine waterfalls, but Mull's most spectacular, Eas Forsa is further up the coastal road, on the way to the Ulva Ferry. Its waters crash down from the high (and dangerous) cliff into a sea pool below. The name is tautological, both words meaning a waterfall, the one in Gaelic, the other in Norse.

The starting point for the expedition which included MacKinnon's Cave was Inch Kenneth, a small island off the southern coast of Loch na Keal, which then belonged to the Macleans. Sir Allan took his guests to see the local oyster beds 'out of which the boatmen forced up as many as were wanted'. Dr Johnson amused himself collecting shells 'picked up for their glossy beauty', but what impressed him most were the chapel, and the ground round it 'covered with grave-stones of Chiefs and ladies'. The chapel, though venerable, was already roofless, but the burial ground was still in use as a place of sepulture. It had long been a staging post for the funeral processions on their way to Iona and when the weather was too rough for the crossing, many of the noble corpses intended for Reilig Oran were laid to rest in Inch Kenneth. 'Inch Kenneth', said Dr Johnson, 'was a proper prelude for Icolmkill (Iona).' The old chapel which he admired is one of many in West Argyll to contain some of the best examples of stone carvings. Though the island is in private hands, permission to visit its ancient monuments can be obtained. In its recent history, Inch Kenneth has been associated with one unpleasant episode – the death of Unity Mitford. One of the famous Mitford sisters, she went to Germany before the Second World War and there developed a 'crush' on Hitler whom she contrived to meet. The Nazi creed was not unfamiliar to the Redesdales – Unity's brother-in-law was Sir Oswald Mosley, leader of the British Fascist movement – and her parents did nothing to discourage her. On the day war was declared in 1939, torn between her feelings for her country and her love for Hitler, she attempted suicide, using a small pistol he had given her. She failed, but damaged her brain irretrievably. A senseless cripple till she died in 1948, she was tended by her mother on Inch Kenneth which Lord Redesdale had bought in 1937.

One of the larger islands off the West Coast, Ulva – with its sister island, Gometra – is also in private hands, but can be visited on application. By some it is remembered chiefly for what it suffered during the Clearances – a population of 800 in 1840 was reduced to 200 by 1850, and soon the island was deserted, its croft houses fallen down and the land gone to waste. Its present owners who breed pedigree cattle and sheep are doing something to repair the damage.

There are other reasons for remembering Ulva, which has both literary and historical associations. In Thomas Campbell's popular ballad, it is the scene of the death of Lord Ullin's daughter. Disapproving of her marriage to a Highland chieftain, Lord Ullin and his men were in hot pursuit of the lovers as they reached the ferry, where they offered the boatman 'a silver pound' to row them across.

'Out spoke the hardy Highland wight,
"I'll go, my chief, I'm ready:
It is not for your silver bright,
But for your winsome lady."'

But a tempest arose, and in the stormy seas, the boat capsized. Lord Ullin reached the shore in time to see his daughter drown; 'his wrath was turned to wailing' as

'The waters wild went o'er his child,
And he was left lamenting.'

The ballad was probably based on a local legend which Campbell would have picked up while he was living at Sunipol, near Calgary, where a local family had engaged him as a tutor.

Ulva has an unexpected connection with feudal marriage customs – the Mencheta Mulierum, under which the Lord of the Manor, in Scotland, the Laird, was entitled to a payment from his tenants on the marriage of their daughters. According to both Johnson and Boswell, the custom, which still survived in their day, had something in common with the ancient code known as Borough English, but they supposed its continued practice was unique to Ulva. Wicked lords having their way with innocent village maidens are the very stuff of romantic novels, but there is no evidence that the 'droit de seigneur' which gave the landowners the right to a girl's maidenhood, was ever enacted. However, the fact that a fine was exacted when a virgin married presupposed some such ancient right. Johnson records that his host on Ulva, 'Mac-Quarry was used to demand a sheep', which was later replaced by a crown, when payment in kind gave way to cash.

Further north and out to sea the twin islands of Coll and Tiree are separated only by the Sound of Gunna, named after the islet between the two. Both are low-lying and rocky, with long sandy beaches, backed by dunes or machair. Their measurements are much the same – about twelve miles long. Coll is roughly three miles wide; Tiree, more deeply indented, varies from a mile and a half to six miles or so. The highest hill on Coll, Ben Hogh, rises to 339 feet; there are two heights at the south-west end of Tiree – Ben Hough, 388 feet and Ben Hynish, which tops 450 feet. A good description of Coll and Tiree was given by Bowman as he viewed them from the deck of the steamer from Tobermory. The first to appear 'right west of us was the long and low isle of Coll stretching along the distant horizon for a considerable space, its red cliffs descending perpendicularly into the ocean, giving it very much the appearance of a long wall. Not a tree was seen upon it. . . . As we pursued our southward track (to Staffa and Iona), the Isle of Tiree appeared very far out to the west; low and dim, but much more level than Coll. Both these islands are of gneiss.' Bowman picked out one of Coll's most spectacular features, the Cairns of Coll, to the north of the island. He saw them as 'a cluster of cliffs consisting of detached rocks, having much the appearance of towering castles whose foundations lie buried beneath the waves'.

The similarity between Coll and Tiree had already been noticed by Martin, who regarded it as providential: 'The Isle of Coll produces more Boys than Girls, and the Isle of Tire-iy more Girls than Boys; as if Nature intended both these Isles for mutual Alliances, without being at the trouble of going to the adjacent Isles or Continent to be matched.' Whether or not modern statistics bear this out, Coll and Tiree continue to form a rather remote community, sharing their isolated corner of the ocean as well as a long and troubled history where legend plays as a big a part as fact. In the days of the Lords of the Isles, both were part of the 'kingdom' of Somerled's son Dugall, then of his son, Duncan. By the middle of the fourteenth century, the Macleans of Duart appeared on the scene, negotiating a settlement with the MacDougalls whom they eventually superseded on both islands. But the Macleans were divided among themselves: the Duarts and the Lochbuies disputed the ownership of their newly acquired territory for another two hundred years. Quarrels between kinsmen are part and parcel of Scottish history, and the tale of how 'Young Col' came to retrieve and secure his inheritance has entered the annals. Boswell came across the story one rainy day he spent

rummaging among old records kept at Breachachadh Castle.

The 'Young Col' in question, Iain Garbh or
Sturdy John, was a fifteenth century ancestor
of Boswell's host. His father died while he
was still an infant and his widowed mother
married the powerful MacNeil of Barra and
settled with him at Grishipoll. By Duart loya-
lists, MacNeil was cast in the role of wicked
stepfather, so they removed young Iain clan-
destinely to Ireland where he grew up in
safety tended by his faithful nurse. When he
reached manhood, he was given to under-
stand that he should return to Coll to fight for
his inheritance. So he sailed for Mull where he
recruited a band of followers from Dervaig.
Among them was the hero of the story – the
Grizzled Lad, Gille Riabhach. The landing

Breachachadh Castle

was achieved without attracting attention, but during the fighting that followed, the Grizzled Lad was hard pressed by one of Mac-Neil's men, known as the Black Tailor, who was armed with a mighty axe. To save his life, the Lad leapt backwards over a burn, then back again to behead his pursuer with his own weapon. The spot where this legendary encounter took place is known as 'the Grizzled Lad's Leap'. The battle ended with young Iain beheading his stepfather and – to make assurance double sure – killing his stepbrother, still a babe in arms. For his part in MacLean's return to Coll, the Lad was rewarded with a grant of land in Dervaig. Not to be outdone, Tiree has a similar story of a giant's leap, marking the spot where a local man chased by a bull jumped 15 feet over a cleft in the cliffs which separates them from an offshore island. The place is known as Sloc a Chain, the Gully of the Leap.

The Macleans continued to hold Coll and Tiree, fighting off occasional raids by the MacDonalds. But they were weakened by clan feuds and having backed the losing side during the Jacobite risings, had eventually to yield to the growing power of the Campbells. So it was left to the Dukes of Argyll to deal with the successive potato famines which struck an economy already weakened by the collapse of the kelp trade and a population decimated by clearances and enforced emigration.

Some of these vicissitudes were in the future when Dr Johnson and Boswell arrived in Coll on a wet October morning in 1773. Time was running short in which to complete their tour and when they left Skye, they intended to make straight for Mull and Iona before rejoining the mainland. But they were caught in a storm off Ardnamurchan – 'a prodigious sea, with immense billows', Boswell called it – and they ran for Coll, landing safely in Loch Eatharna (Lochiern to Boswell). Two days later, the weather had mended, the wind stood fair for Mull but, as Dr Johnson said, "having . . . landed on a new Island, we would not leave it wholly unexamined'. In the end, they spent about ten days on Coll, most of the time as the guests of Donald Maclean, the 'Young Col' of the day, at Breachachadh New Castle. As they saw it – minus its pepper pot towers – it was 'a neat gentleman's residence' built in 1750 by Hector Maclean alongside the old buildings which remain one of the best examples of a fifteenth century west coast castle. It was here that Dr Johnson listened to Maclean's plans and praised 'his very laudable desire of improving his patrimony' by planting an orchard where 'no attempt has yet been made to raise a tree' and, more realistically perhaps, by introducing the cultivation of turnips to provide winter fodder for the cattle. Dr Johnson had his own suggestions to make which included stocking the island's many lochs and rivers which already contained trout and eels so that fish would always be available even when the sea was too rough for the boats to set out. And much as he had suffered from the weather himself, he noted that the harvest ripened earlier in Coll than in Skye, and that the winters were never cold. During his peregrinations through the island mounted on a sheltie, a little Highland steed which he described as 'very low' but unexpectedly 'musculous and sturdy', he noted with approval places where the heath had been reclaimed for corn and pasture; he also came across the phenomenon known as sandblow, sand shifted by gale force winds which move whole dunes over the grass lands and even threaten the crofters' houses. Still, he shared Maclean's belief that much could be done for Coll, and for Tiree which he regarded as 'eminent for its fertility', and consequently so 'well peopled' that a company of nine hundred and fourteen had attended a funeral there.

Tiree, as we now call it, rivals Iona in the variety of names it has been given and the number of ways they have been spelt. One of the oldest is Tir–I, the land of corn, which suggests that it once served as breadbasket to Columba's flock on Iona. According to Dean Munro's account, 'na cuntrie may be mair fertile of corn, and very good for wild fowls and fische'. Shooting parties out after snipe in Tiree will not argue.

VII
Days out in Dalriada

Ships on their way back from Coll and Tiree,
generally via Tobermory, give passengers a
sight of two more islands, Kerrera and Lismore, and pass by a small speck in the Sound,
known as the Lady's Rock, where the long
and bloody history of the Macleans and the
Campbells come together. The rivalry between the two feuding clans is interspersed
with attempts at reconciliation: in one such,
the Lady Elizabeth Campbell, the beautiful
daughter of the Earl of Argyll – for the
daughters of great chieftains are always beautiful – was married off to the widowed Laird
of Duart, Lachlan Maclean. It was a forced
marriage which did not work out and Maclean, displeased with his newly wedded wife,
isolated her from her family lest she should
complain. Some say this was because she had
failed to give him an heir; others, that she had
lost her heart and remained faithful to an English lover, Sir Malise Graeme, a friend of her
brother, Lord Lorne. However that may be,
Maclean decided to dispose of his unsatisfac-
tory wife. And so she was taken at dead of
night to a rock off Duart Castle which was
immersed at high tide. As the waters rose, she
was spotted and rescued. There are various
accounts of who her saviours were, but all
agree that she was taken back in secret to
Inveraray where her father exacted a bloody

retribution. Confident that his wife was drowned, the Laird of Duart had set out for Inveraray to bring the Earl the sad news that his daughter had taken ill and died. The Earl kept quiet, receiving his son-in-law with all the kindness due to a grieving widower. A fine banquet was spread out for his refreshment – at which the Lady Elizabeth appeared. Maclean was cut down as he tried to escape. Further details – as to whether the lady then married Graeme, for instance – are best left to academics, and the precise location of the rock on which she nearly met her death, to geographers.

Another young lady associated with the Macleans is remembered in Lismore where a well is named after her, Tobar a Clar. Doña Clara, the daughter of a Spanish grandee and a close relation of King Philip's, would have nothing to do with her many suitors dreaming of a tall, fair young man with blue eyes with whom she had fallen in love. Such looks belong to northern climes rather than to sunburnt Spain and, in pursuit of her dream Doña Clara took passage on the *Florida*. As the Seanachie, or bard, tells it, she may well had been the reason why the ship was mysteriously blown up. For Lachlan Maclean, Lord of Duart, answered Doña Clara's vision perfectly. His lady soon came to suspect that the Spaniard was the cause of her husband's many and prolonged visits to the ship at anchor in Tobermory Bay. And so – possibly with the help of the great witch who lived on Ben More – Lady Maclean planned the explosion which sent the *Florida* to the bottom. Lachlan had left when she blew up; he was the only survivor. The crew and its captain lay trapped in the ship, but Doña Clara's corpse floated free and was carried to Lismore where she was buried near the site of St Moluag's settlement. But she could not rest in peace. One night she appeared to Lachlan in a dream, demanding that he should wash her bones in the waters of the well nearby and take them back to Spain. And this, says the Seanachie, was done.

The main landmark on Kerrera is a modern one – a fine obelisk erected to the founder of Caledonian – MacBrayne. Further back in time and at the other end of the island stand the impressive ruins of Castle Gylen, a stronghold of the MacDougalls which was virtually destroyed during the wars of the Covenant. There is a tradition that Alexander II, on his way to reduce the Western Islands, died here (in 1249) of a fever – or perhaps by poison. Once Kerrera provided extra pasture for cattle from Mull; nowadays it is the perfect setting for a sunny day spent between sea and sky with only the occasional sheep for company.

In a country of castles, one of the most important is Dunstaffnage on the outskirts of Oban. First seen from the road through the masts and rigging of the yachts and small craft which crowd the new marina in the bay, it was built in the 13th century. Its thick curtain walls punctuated by towers rise from a rocky promontory at the mouth of Loch

Etive. The tower house belongs to the seventeenth century, but the adjoining chapel dates back to the twelve hundreds. A position of such strategic importance may well have tempted the Vikings, as later it did the MacDougalls. But the site the castle occupies goes back in history much further – as traditional guardian of the Stone of Destiny, it may have replaced Dunadd (near Crinan) as the capital of the ancient kingdom of Dalriada. Founded late in the fifth century by Fergus MacErc, who came from Ireland to join his fellow countrymen already settled on the West coast, it lasted until 843 when Kenneth MacAlpin succeeded in subduing the Picts and bringing a measure of unification to the territories north of the Forth. The Stone, brought to Scotland by Fergus and lodged at Dunadd or Dunstaffnage and probably both, continued to play its part in the royal ceremonial as it had done in the inauguration of Irish kings. When Kenneth MacAlpin moved his capital east to Dunkeld, near Perth, he took the stone with him and lodged it at Scone – the name by which it is generally known. There it remained until Edward the First marked his victory over the Scots in 1296 by removing it to Westminster where it forms part of the Coronation Chair. The MacDougalls were in possession of another royal treasure – the so-called Brooch of Lorn, which had belonged to Robert the Bruce. As the story goes, the Bruce, hard pressed in battle by the MacDougalls, was able to escape only by ripping his cloak and leaving the brooch that secured it in

their hands. It consists of a large quartz surrounded by a circlet of pearls.

In the fourteenth century the MacDougalls gave way to the Stewarts of Lorn who made Dunstaffnage their principal seat. There a dispute broke out with the Campbells of Argyll as to who was the rightful heir, and John of Lorn was murdered, cut down on his way to Dunstaffnage chapel where he was about to marry the mother of his illegitimate son. The dispute dragged on ending in a complicated compromise and eventually Dunstaffnage went to the Earls, then Dukes of Argyll. The great castle continued to make its mark on history: through the centuries it survived many skirmishes and sieges; after Prince Charles Edward's escape, Flora MacDonald spent a night there on her way to London and imprisonment in the Tower; the famous visited it, it was painted by Turner rising through the mist across the water. But tourists interested in the castle's history are probably far outnumbered by those who come to enjoy the magnificent scenery of sea and lochs, moor and mountain, in which it stands.

Close at hand are the Falls of Lara – rapids seen at their spectacular best at low tide in the spring. The whole region is associated with Deirdre of the Sorrows, the beautiful daughter of an old Irish harper who was discovered and courted by the King of Ulster, but fell in love with Naoise, one of three brothers in the King's entourage. To escape the King's wrath, they made their way to Scotland where they lived happily together for a few years – the old hill fort on the northern shores of Loch Etive is called after them, the Dun of the Sons of Usna. The story, which was told in the days of Cuchullin, has an unhappy ending: through trickery and magic, Naoise and his brothers all met their death and Deirdre killed herself for love.

From mythology to modern times – a fine bridge at Connel crosses the narrows near the entrance to the loch. It was built between 1898 and 1903, a close contemporary of the Firth of Forth bridge which celebrated its centenary in 1990, to carry the railway which ran from Oban to Ballachulish; a footbridge was added later. At the other end of the loch before it turns to bite deep into the hills, the villages for Taynuilt and Bonawe mark the entrance to the Pass of Brander where Robert the Bruce won a notable victory against the MacDougalls in 1308. It is a gloomy, treeless defile which joins Loch Etive to Loch Awe. It is overlooked by one of the mountains which dominate the district, Ben Cruachan, where several peaks rise to over 3,000 feet. They say that it was the swirling mists from the mountain which, by hiding Bruce and his men from the enemy, helped him win the day. Since 1965, however, Ben Cruachan has been a source of light for it houses a power station which is generally praised as a feat of engineering. The mountain is hollowed out to house the machine hall, reached by a mile-long tunnel excavated from solid rock. The turbines which are reversible pump the waters of Loch Awe up into a reservoir high on a corrie on the mountain's side. The station produces 450 million units of electricity a year.

Loch Awe, Scotland's longest loch stretching out for 25 miles, is in the very heart of the kingdom of Dalriada which became Argyle. A land of lochs and forests, its coastline reaches 140 miles north from the Mull of Kintyre to Loch Linnhe, taking in Lorn, Morvern and Ardnamurchan. While the MacDonalds held the Lordship of the Isles, the Campbells fought them for supremacy, then played a full if varied part in the affairs of the Crown. Apart from the local feuds, there were Campbells at all the major engagements, sometimes on one side, sometimes on the other, occasionally on both. Sir Colin Campbell, the progenitor of the Campbells of Argyll was knighted in 1280; he was the first to receive the appellation of MacCailean Mor which successive chiefs have since used. The earldom was created in 1457, the dukedom dates back to William of Orange. When Dutch William landed in November 1688, a Campbell was at hand, Archibald, the 10th Earl, soon to become the first Duke. It was with the new dynasty, in which Stuart blood was running thin, that the Campbells came into their own, joining the great Lowland families in their absolute allegiance to the English throne.

The Stuart cause was given up for good, and in the long run local loyalties made way for politics, though the Campbells remained proud of their ancient, romantic origins. Sporting a boar's head as their crest, they claim descent from the legendary Diarmid, the great hunter. It was Diarmid, Fingal's companion, who killed the Boar of Caledonia. The bards have sung of the fearsome battle in which he tackled the beast single-handed, slew it, then died himself, perhaps through the connivance of secret enemies, when he trod on the boar and one of its poisonous bristles pricked his foot. This was in the days when the Great Caledonian Forest covered the country, so the mortal combat between Diarmid and the boar may just as well have taken place near Loch Awe as elsewhere. At any rate, it is remembered there.

The Great Forest has gone, but the shores of Loch Awe are still beautifully wooded with columns of Caledonian pine, birch, oak and ash. The availability of so much timber in the district made Taynuilt and Bonawe the centre of iron-smelting as early as Elizabethan times, and extensive ironworks were established there in the eighteenth century.

The three lochs, Awe, Etive and Fyne,

which gives Argyle its main outlet to the sea, are at the very heart of Campbell country, with Oban as a good centre for visiting the two places most closely associated with them – their capital, Inveraray, and Glencoe, the site of the 'massacre' which is remembered as one of the darkest incidents in Scottish history.

Travelling north along the coast road to Ballachulish, where another modern bridge (1976) replaces the ferry across Loch Leven, we rejoin Robert Louis Stevenson in Appin. Only a few small townships maintain a link with the famous, and still unsolved, murder mystery, notably Duror and Kentalban where the victim Colin Campbell, the Red Fox, was shot dead and Acharn, the home of James Stewart, the man who was hanged for the murder. In 'Kidnapped', the story is told to David Balfour by another of the book's heroes, Alan Breck, "the speckled one", who in real life was a Stewart outlaw who had contrived to come and go between the exiled Stuart court in France and the Highlands ever since the collapse of the '45. His name was Allan Stewart; he acquired his Gaelic nickname of 'speckled' or 'spotted' from the smallpox which had marked him in childhood. He tells his story from the point of view of the dispossessed members of his clan: 'Ye ken very well', he says, 'that I am an Appin Stewart, and the Campbells have long harried and wasted those of my name; ay, and got land from us by treachery – but never by the sword.' Colin Campbell was the Argyll factor appointed to manage the forfeited estates, among them those of Stewart of Ardsheal and Cameron of Lochiel. As was usual in those days, he had family connections on both sides, and modern opinion has vindicated him to the extent of believing that he made his rule as tolerant as he could. Nevertheless, James Stewart, 'of the Glen' as he was known, had suffered under it. He was among the many whom Alan Breck had seen reduced to 'buying butter in the market place, and taking it home in a kale (cabbage) leaf'.

There were several suspects when the Red Fox was killed in the woods of Lettermore. Alan Breck himself confessed to the murder, but he was ignored since there was already a price on his head. James Stewart was arrested, imprisoned at Fort William, taken to Inveraray to be tried before a jury consisting mainly of Campbells and hanged at Ballachulish in November 1752. According to the grim custom of the day, his body was left hanging in its chains. But there is a story that it was removed by two local brothers, named Livingstone, who gave it a decent burial, then fled to Ulva where they settled as crofters.

There are few landmarks connected with the Appin murder, but James' family, the Stewarts of Appin, descendants of that Stewart of Lorn who was murdered at Dunstaffnage, have a splendid memorial in their ancient fortress Castle Stalker. Built offshore round about 1500 where little Loch Laich meets Loch Linnhe, it dominates the multitude of tiny islets which surround it – one of

the nicest examples of those Scottish castles which replaced a defensive moat by the waters of sea or loch.

A great deal of research has gone into the Appin murder, but without much result; millions of words, gallons of ink, tons of paper, miles of typewriter ribbon have been used up on the Glencoe massacre. In both cases, details have been established, but motives are more refractory and remain open to speculation. The events leading up to the killings in the Pass of Glencoe – on a dark winter's morning in 1692 – are plain enough. King William had offered the Highland leaders an amnesty if they took an oath of allegiance to

Castle Stalker

him not later than the 1st of January. Some submitted, others hesitated, among them the chief of a sept of Clan MacDonald, MacIan MacDonald of Glencoe. Just before the deadline expired, he decided to give in and rode off through the snow to Inverlochy, near Fort William, only to be sent on to Inveraray where his oath was taken and accepted as valid on 6th January. A letter to this effect was sent to Edinburgh. Considering himself under safe-conduct, MacIan made his way back to Glencoe where a company of Government troops was being quartered on his people. Their commander, Captain Robert Campbell of GlenLyon, a relative by marriage, stayed with MacIan and his sons; the troops found billets with the clansmen. There are many accounts of fraternising till, at dawn on the 13th of February, the troops carried out orders received from their superior officer, a Major Duncannon, to: 'fall upon the MacDonalds of Glencoe and put all to the sword under seventy; you are to have a special care that the old fox and his sons doe on no account escape your hands'. In all, less than forty MacDonalds were killed, though more may have died as they tried to escape through the mist on to the frozen moor. Their homes were burnt down, their cattle driven off; MacIan himself was shot dead by one of his guests – for so he regarded the officers staying with him.

And that is why Glencoe has never been forgotten – no mere clan feud, but a breach of the sacred laws of hospitality, unforgivable in the Highlands.

Who picked MacIan and his small clan as a victim, whether this monstrous act of retribution was planned in Edinburgh, or in London or nearer to home, at Inveraray, will probably never be known. In defence of the Campbells, it is said that the Earl of Argyll was furious when he heard the news. It is said too that once the Campbell troops in the glen had received their orders for the slaughter, they did all they could to give warning – and the relatively small number of the dead gives some credence to this. But the doings on that grim February day have left their mark on folk memory and influenced generations of tourists to regard Glencoe as forbidding. It has been much visited, and written up, by travellers who made what amounts to a pilgrimage there. They include the historian, Thomas Babington Macaulay, Dorothy Wordsworth and Charles Dickens, who found it 'perfectly terrible. The pass is an awful place'. Bowman, who spoke of the 'interminable ocean of billowing hills which everywhere met the eye', thought it 'the most dreadful and desolate glen in Scotland'. Earlier (1769), Thomas Pennant had called it 'infamous for the massacre of its inhabitants', and picking up a piece of folklore, 'celebrated for having (as some assert) given birth to Ossian'. Otherwise, he was more interested in the oats and barley its four hundred inhabitants farmed and in the 'black' cattle they raised. He made a careful note of what shooting the neighbourhood provided – red deer, Alpine hare, ptarmigan, moor-fowl and some partridge only recently introduced. But his was not yet the age of sensibility. The scenery, however, is certainly grandiose and if Glencoe is approached from the east by Rannoch Moor – itself a high plateau of peat bogs and lochans as desolate as a lunar landscape – the general impression it gives may well be gloomy. For travellers from Oban, carrying on inland from Ballachulish, it may present a more pleasing aspect. In William Daniell's landscape, taken from across Loch Leven, clear cut, sunlit mountains, their lower slopes rosy with heather, overlook the quiet waters of the lake busy with ferry and fishing boats.

Glencoe

These are the waters that Captain Campbell
and his Redcoats crossed to occupy Glencoe.
But as John Prebble, the modern authority on
the massacre, points out, 'Unlike others who
have put this valley on paper or canvas,
Daniell did not feel obliged to convey the
horror of the winter night that made it the
best-known of all Highland glens.' On a fine
day in Glencoe, as it narrows and winds away
east, the sun catches rags of snow gleaming
on the heights, and brightens the grass by the
river that foams white over the pebbles. As
sheep graze along the stretch of water mea-
dow, it is a quiet, pastoral scene in which the
ghosts of Campbells and MacDonalds fade

away. But it is surrounded by some of the most forbidding mountains in Scotland – the Buchailles (or shepherds) of Etive, guarding the entrance to the Glen, and the Three Sisters, outliers of the great Bidean nam Bian range, which rises to not far from 4,000 feet. It may be that people get from Glencoe what they bring to it: its magnificent scenery inspires some to remember, and some to forget, the 'far off things, and battles long ago'.

The place where it all started, Inveraray, capital of the Argylls, is less controversial, a charming Georgian town on the banks of Loch Fyne, about three-quarters of a mile below the castle. Its white-washed houses, replacing the huddle of medieval dwellings clustered round the Campbells' ancient fortress, have changed very little since they were built in mid-eighteenth century. They include a fine inn, the Argyll Arms, and a church remarkable for being divided into two parts so that separate services could be held concurrently in English and Gaelic without the congregations mixing. Pennant was at Inveraray when the 'new town' was being built: 'This place will in time be very magnificent: but at present the space between the front and the water is disgraced with the old town, composed of the most wretched hovels that can be imagined. The founder of the castle designed to have built a new town on the west side of the little bay the house stands on: he finished a few houses, a custom-house, and an excellent inn.' All were laid out by the architects, the most prominent of their time, who were at work on the castle, which Archibald, the third Duke, decided to rebuild in modern style in 1743. Started soon after the Forty-Five, it took twelve years to complete and old prints show it, standing four-square in its parkland, with its corner towers and crenellations as an early example of the Gothic Revival. Its present aspect is more elaborate, some may say fussy, with a profusion of conical spires added after a fire in 1877. A more recent fire, in 1975, did severe damage to the upper stories and destroyed many works of art. Inveraray Castle is on most tourist itineraries – and for those who are disappointed by its exterior, there is the magnificent interior to admire. Planned late in the eighteenth century by the fifth Duke, it was modelled on Carlton House, the London residence of the Prince Regent, which it rivals in the splendour of its decoration. Under the famous plasterwork ceilings, furniture of the day in the French style, a gallery of Beauvais tapestries, a collection of porcelain complete the general effect. The armoury hall, reaching up past the pipers' gallery, to the roof, is a reminder of earlier, more bloodthirsty times. Dr Johnson 'took much notice of the large collection of arms, which are excellently displayed' when he had the satisfaction of dining with the Duke. The Duke extended his kindness further: he mounted Johnson on a 'stately steed' from his stables – a pleasant change, no doubt, from the shelties which had carried the Doctor throughout his Scottish journeyings. He also supplied 'conveniences for surveying the spacious park and rising forests'. So Dr Johnson was able to drive through the Castle grounds in 'a low one-horse chair' and Boswell took 'a particular pride in shewing him a great number of fine old trees, to compensate for the nakedness which had made such an impression on him on the eastern coast of Scotland'. Thirty years later, another English traveller, Thomas Thornton was writing of these same trees. 'The woods around are very extensive, as are those near the house. The trees, many of which bear marks of high antiquity, are chiefly beech; there are also some oaks, chestnuts, and ash, with a few others, as the plane and silver fir; these variegated with thriving plantation, beautifully diversify the rides around this charming spot.' Thornton's hobby was shooting, but in his letters from Scotland, his eye for game extended to their habitat. He was less concerned with his human surroundings. He described Inveraray Castle in some detail, but without much comment, and thought little of the town – 'it is hardly worth notice', he says. It was obviously the woodland that appealed to him, as it does to the many modern travellers who stroll through the castle grounds and along the banks of the river Aray (or Ara) up to the bridge, with its triple arches, which was designed by one of the castle's chief architects, Robert Mylne.

Johnson and Boswell came to Inveraray at the very end of their Scottish tour – with Loch Lomond, it was their last stop on the way home. The visit was an unqualified success from the start when they arrived at the inn which Dr Johnson found 'not only commodious, but magnificent'. It was here, by the way, that he tasted whisky for the first and only time and declared it 'preferable to any English malt brandy'. Pennant, too, found the inn 'excellent'. Only Robert Burns criticised it, leaving behind this inscription:

'There's nothing here but Hielan' pride
An' Hielan scab, an' hunger;
If providence has sent me here
T'were surely in his anger.'

But then Burns was a Lowlander, and very likely in his cups. Bowman liked the Argyll

Arms so well that he even tackled the national dish – a sheep's head – with apparent equanimity.

Bowman explored Inveraray from top to bottom, taking long walks by the side of the loch and along the river, admiring the effect of the sunset on the waters. He was among those energetic enough to climb the high hill of Duniquoich (700 feet), up through the trees to the old watch tower at the summit. The tower he found 'unsightly' but the modern eye may see its square simplicity as a pleasing contrast to the elaboration of the present day castle. It was one of the many which served medieval Scotland as part of an elaborate advance warning system.

On the way back from Inveraray along Loch Awe, the Castle of Kilchurn rises from flat marshland under the shadow of Ben Cruachan. It was built in 1440 by Sir Colin Campbell of Glenorchy, the progenitor of the Breadalbane branch. Towards the end of the seventeenth century, the first Earl extended the keep. But the castle was subsequently abandoned as the family moved east into Tayside. One of its towers was blown down in the great gale of 1879. But the fine gateway is intact, surmounted by the Earl's coat of arms. It stands as one more reminder of the Argyll's longevity, power and influence.

VIII

'The Greater Your Esteem'

It was of Inveraray Castle and its policies that James Hogg wrote 'the closer the inspection, the more exalted your admiration; and the better acquaintance, the greater your esteem.' Though sheep farming had been his main concern in the days he spent there, the Ettrick shepherd – with an eye to future publication – turned man of letters in the account of his travels he gave to Walter Scott. What he said of Inveraray holds good for many places, but with the Western Highlands there is this one difference – it is generally love at first sight.

The scheduled services by sea from Glasgow are a thing of the past: nowadays tourists reach Oban and Mull by road or rail. And since for many of them Glasgow (or Edinburgh) is already a long way from home, the train is often the most popular option. The journey down Clydebank – a slow one with many stops – provides a sorry reminder of industrial decay, but once past Dumbarton and heading north, some of the most spectacular scenery in Scotland comes into view. It is hard to forget one's first sight of Loch Lomond, lying still and deep and solitary between its high and heavily wooded banks, under the shadow of Ben Lomond, the peak that gives it its modern name. The train runs along the western shore of the Loch for the whole of its length, 26 miles, then travels north along Glen Falloch in Breadalbane country to the main junction at Crianlarich, the tiny, isolated 'railway town' which serves the north-west. There is a pause and time to stretch one's legs before the train divides to carry passengers to Oban, west along the Grampians. This is pastoral country, through Glen Lochy whose river meets the waters of the Orchy on their way down from the north. The journey continues by the Pass of Brander along a short arm of Loch Awe to Taynuilt and Loch Etive, and a final short lap by Connel brings it to its end in Oban.

The journey from London to Oban can be made in a day, but not to Mull for as the train draws into the station, the last ferry from the adjoining pier is already well on its way. There are no guaranteed connections, and as long as British and Scottish Rail continue to cold-shoulder each other, travellers from the south will be condemned to make the last part of the beautiful journey after dark. Since trains from all but the north of England leave too late for passengers to catch the mid-morning train in Glasgow, the alternative is to spend a night there, or in Edinburgh, or in one of the border towns, so as to be able to enjoy the journey through the Highlands by daylight and reach Oban in time to cross to Mull. On the other hand, it is no hardship to follow the example of travellers in the past and spend the night there, to wake to the rewards of a Scottish breakfast before joining the crowd on the quay, there to acquire the current Caledonian-MacBrayne timetables.

The ferries cross to Mull every two hours on average, starting early – at seven or eight o'clock – on weekdays, and there are Sunday sailings too. The last ferry to Craignure leaves Oban at 1900 in summer; the last from the island crosses it. Local buses meet most ferries at Craignure to take passengers by road to Tobermory (or put them down anywhere on the way at their request); during the tourist season, it is occasionally possible to sail from Oban to Tobermory direct. And motorists on Mull are well served by the car ferry, also operated by 'Cal-Mac', which runs hourly from Fishnish to Lochaline. Ferries to Lismore operate from the main quay in Oban; the service to Kerrera has its own jetty on the southern outskirts of Oban. The summer service, the fullest, comes into operation in mid-May, ending with September; the winter service, much reduced, is tailored to the needs of residents, the high-school children, workers on the mainland, shoppers from Mull. The off-lying islands, which depend on the ferries for their supplies, continue to be served. But getting to them, even in summer, requires some planning. Coll and Tiree, for instance, can be reached within the day, but there is little time – no more than an hour – to explore them. It is also possible to sail to Colonsay: there are evening trips down through the Firth of Lorn with its technicolour sunsets and out to sea past the Garvellachs which seem to lie on the very edge of the world. But the ferry makes its forty mile trip without docking at Scalasaig. Once a week, however, an afternoon ferry takes over passengers intending to spend a few days on the island. Colonsay, whose nearest neighbour is Islay, is generally associated through its history and geography with the group of Hebridean islands known collectively as the 'smaller isles'. About 8 miles long and 3 miles across at its widest, it is fairly typical of the Outer Hebrides, with fine sand beaches and stretches of machair. It is flat, but not treeless – birch and oak survive, as well as such natives as rowan and hazel and willow. Colonsay House stands in the valley of Kiloran, which is protected from the Atlantic blasts by a high coastal escarpment. Its tropical gardens are considered to be among the finest in Scotland. Electricity has only recently come to Colonsay, and with it more visitors than its population of crofters have seen in generations. But Colonsay was a centre of mediaeval culture when Oronsay Priory was built towards the end of the fourteenth century. Despoiled during the Reformation, its ruins remain impressive. They include the remains of a fine cloister and a beautiful free-standing stone cross – some rank them second only to Iona. They are reached at low tide across the muddy flats which join Oronsay to Colonsay's south-east coast.

Some of the mini-cruises from Oban – to Iona, for instance, and Staffa – run in conjunction with the local coach operators who collect passengers at Craignure and take them across Mull to their next port of embarkation. The coach offices, from where tours on the mainland leave, are all in the centre of Oban, near the pier and the train station, and a very short distance from Argyle Square where the invaluable Tourist Information Centre occupies the site of Dr Johnson's 'tolerable inn'.

Year in, year out, Caledonian-Macbrayne, the main artery of circulation in West Coast waters, serves a total of twenty-three islands, ferrying both passengers and supplies from the mainland. For tourists, the system is complemented by private companies, whose itineraries are planned to suit special interests. The range is wide: from bird-watching from a motor-boat weaving its way round Staffa and Coll and the Treshnish Islands, home of the puffin, in waters frequented by the occasional whale and dolphin; gastronomy enjoyed during several days at sea aboard a luxury liner which boasts a cuisine based on fresh local produce, or the simple pleasures of an afternoon's sailing (from Taynuilt) on Loch Etive to enjoy the grandiose view of mountain and moor seen from the water. There can be few holiday-makers who do not find opportunities to pursue their hobby, and since this is Scotland, golfers are well catered for. Anglers are spoilt. Mull alone has at least six rivers and lochs well stocked with salmon and trout; on the mainland, Loch Awe and Loch Etive are among the many frequented by fishermen. Most fishing is protected but permits are readily available. Sea angling trips are popular, too.

Planning the next day's outing, on an evening spent surrounded by guide books and timetables, is for me one of the most agreeable of post-prandial occupations. Motorists, incidentally, should be careful to check whether they can take their cars with them since some of the smaller islands, Iona for instance, ban all drivers who are not on essential business. The weather is always a consideration, and choosing the time of year comes first when planning the whole journey. Though Mull is quite a long way up in the northern half of the British Isles, its climate is unexpectedly temperate. The winter is admittedly a long one, and even in spring, snow may fall on fields thick with daffodils. In the outlying islands, which come under the influence of the Gulf Stream, the climate is milder still: on Mull, rhododendrons and azaleas flourish in season; on Colonsay, bamboo and palm trees grow in the open in the gardens of Kiloran. On a July day, Bowman recorded 'intense heat' on Iona where the temperature was 82° Fahrenheit and the summer can produce days when the sea turns a Mediterranean blue. It can also produce days of sheeting rain, but less perhaps of the thick Highland mist which so often blocks out the view elsewhere in the Hebrides. Waterproof clothing, however, is a must, and stout shoes rather than summer sandals which soon come to grief on sea-washed gangways and decks.

The season proper in Oban starts in mid-May with a festival of Highlands and Islands music and dance, where chiefs foregather while their pipers keep the old tradition alive with the martial airs to which the clansmen marched into battle and the laments which marked their deaths, and fiddlers recreate the merriment which accompanied weddings and ceilidh gatherings round the peat fire. Not to be outdone, Mull too has its musical events running through most of April and centred on Tobermory and Dervaig. In 1990, Mendelssohn and his memories of Staffa were the main theme and hundreds of early trippers and tourists were treated to the unusual sight of a string orchestra playing on the sands. Dervaig itself has an unusual attraction – the Little Theatre with its forty-three seats packed into an old converted barn on the road to Salen. Founded in 1966, with its own company, it features in the Guinness Book of Records as the smallest professional theatre in the world. Highland Games continue to be held, with massed pipe bands playing on as kilted athletes compete in tossing the caber, putting the shot, throwing the hammer – ancient sports some dating back to the eleventh century when such displays of skill and strength could lead to promotion in the army. The season ends on a more modern note with the Mull Car Rally which is held in October. Within a week or so, the ferries revert to their off-peak service, hotel bookings drop away (many of the smaller hotels close for a month or two during the winter), the thriving bed-and-breakfast trade dwindles, all but the biggest Tourist Information Centres shut up shop, and the islanders, bidding farewell to their annual guests, revert to an older, quieter routine. Summer is the time for sport and outdoor activities; winter has its many beauties, but the lack of communication and the hazards of driving – gales, roads closed by drifting snow, avalanches – deter all but the hardiest travellers and those on business or duty-bound. Perhaps the best time to enjoy the West Coast and its islands is in spring, as the snows melt, and the mountainside glitters with rushing waters and the machair spreads itself out in full flower, or the autumn, when the heather on the moor comes into its own.

Whenever they may choose to go, holiday-makers are always dependent on the weather – those days seem endless when the rain splashes down along the hotel windows and sullen storm clouds occlude the view. But in Oban, at any rate, there is generally something to do, including a visit to the famous Sea-Life centre (at Barcaldine, about 10 miles north) where all of the marine world from seals to starfish and sea-urchins seems to be on display.

There is one pleasure always to be had whatever the weather or the time of year, the pleasure provided by the Scottish table. Given its harsh climate and unyielding soil, the variety of foodstuffs Scotland produces is truly astonishing. Time was when even modest landowners could live, and live well, off their own estates, in luxury according to Elizabeth Grant of Rothiemurchus. Writing in 1812, she describes the household's common fare: 'Game was plentiful, red-deer, roe, hares, grouse, ptarmigan and partridge; the rivers provided trout and salmon, the different lochs pike and char; the garden abounded in common fruits and common vegetables; cranberries and raspberries ran over the country, and the poultry yard was well furnished.' Scotland is still famous for its raspberries, though canning and freezing, taking up whole crops bought in advance, has reduced the availability of fresh fruit; the quantity of game freshly shot for the table has been curtailed since so much of it is protected by big business for the sake of the very profitable sport it provides. The snipe which Thomas Thornton enjoyed at an inn on Tayside in 1804 are now hard to come by; they were served as part of a second course consisting of brandered chicken and cold ham, washed down by 'good' port and claret and 'incomparable' porter. The crofter's resources were obviously less than his chief's, but the tradition of hospitality – and keeping a good table was part of it – was just as strong. Travelling in the Outer Hebrides, Alexander Carmichael, the nineteenth century authority on Gaelic lore, was invited to sit down to fried herrings and turbot 'fresh from the sea', eggs and butter and cream, scones and bannocks and oatcakes.

Thornton's lavish meal started with a hodge-podge, the local word for the thick stew of vegetables and whatever meat may be available which the French call 'hochepot'. Students of gastronomy often find a French influence in the care the Scots take over the humblest ingredients, and the many words concerned with food and its preparation which are derived from the French lend substance to the theory. Haggis itself is said to be a mispronunciation of 'hachis', the French word for mince; the leg of mutton displayed in the butcher's window may still be labelled 'gigot', the dish on which it was served up was known as an ashet (from 'assiette'); the kitchen utensils, the French 'batterie de cuisine', were referred to as a battery, cinnamon was known as canel, or 'canelle', and the liquid measure called a chopin is derived from 'chopine', the Old French equivalent of half-a-litre. The 'silver tassie' from which Burns drank his pint of wine is merely the French tasse.

Scotland has had close links with France since the Auld Alliance was forged in 1165; France remained an ally while England became the hereditary enemy. There was a constant traffic between Scotland and the continent, and plenty of opportunities to absorb French manners and customs, as well as the language. The Scottish royal family had its share of French blood: Mary Queen of Scots, and Queen of France for a short while, was half-French through her mother, Marie de Guise. And when newly-widowed, she returned to Edinburgh to reclaim her Scottish inheritance, all things French became the fashion. Mary came back surrounded by attendants homesick for France and eager to introduce to the cold and gloomy Scottish capital some of the luxury and light-heartedness they had enjoyed at the Valois court. The French tendency was kept up by the Jacobites, but how far it spread beyond court circles and how much it affected the people is hard to say. What the French and the Scots have in common, however, is the pride they take in their national larder. Whatever it may contain, they make the most of it. In spite of the inroads made by 'fast food', many hotels and bars and restaurants still give priority to fresh produce – soups are home-made and a proper pleasure is taken in dishing up the local shellfish.

Some say the best meal of all is breakfast – a truly Scottish feast which owes nothing to the continent, whether or not it starts with porridge. Whatever the day may bring, here is a chance to enjoy the famous Loch Fyne kippers, small and plump and juicy, or a piece of creamy Finnan haddock, surmounted by a poached egg as plat de resistance, or, for its amateurs, the local black pudding which comes with crispy Ayrshire bacon cut thin from the collar. Dr Johnson knew well what he was talking about when he said that 'if an epicure could remove by a wish, in quest of sensual gratification, wherever he had supped he would breakfast in Scotland'.

Fish must figure largely in gastronomic experiences on Mull and the islands, in Oban and its neighbourhood. As anglers know, there is nothing better than brown trout from the burn dusted with oatmeal and grilled or a cut of fresh salmon gently poached and served with a home-made mayonnaise or Hollandaise sauce. Such dishes are memorable, and to recall them Mrs Prunella Kilbane has again been kind enough to give me some of the fish dishes from an international collection which the clients of her restaurants and her many grateful friends have enjoyed.

These recipes are for four persons, except where otherwise stated.

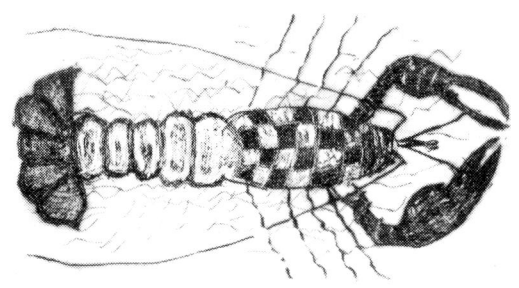

Bisque of Shellfish

The basis of all Bisques is a well seasoned, dry white wine court-bouillon, in which the fish has been allowed to marinate overnight. When well made, it is an epicure's delight.

Ingredients

a) Marinade:

3 pts white wine
½ pt wine vinegar
3 dsps olive oil
Juice of half a lemon
½ a carrot (peeled)

1 onion (chopped)
2 shallots (chopped)
White part of a leek (chopped)
Clove of garlic (peeled and crushed)
3 bay leaves
Ground black pepper and salt
4 sprigs of parsley

b) Bisque:

2 lbs chosen fish
3 lbs tomatoes
6 fld oz good sherry
10 fld oz double cream
3 beaten egg yolks

Method

The day before, prepare the marinade, shell the fish and marinate overnight.

Next day chop the tomatoes, transfer the fish in its marinade to a saucepan, add tomatoes and simmer gently until cooked. Allow to cool.

Remove fish and tomatoes and put through blender. Replace this mixture in the marinade and allow to simmer for 1½ hours. Then strain. Just before serving beat the egg yolks and add to the liquid together with the cream and the sherry. Stir well and serve.

It is no good making a small quantity of this soup. The above recipe will make enough for eight and it is so good that I have no doubt your guests will ask for a second helping or certainly want it served again the following day!

Grilled Mackerel

Mackerel has such a good flavour when it is really fresh (don't eat it if it isn't) that I think it is a shame to cover it in a rich sauce. So here is a simple way of getting the best taste out of it.

Ingredients

1 mackerel per person
The juice of a lemon
1 lemon (cut into wedges for the garnish)
1 tbs chopped fresh parsley
4 tbs butter (one for each fish)
Freshly ground black pepper

Method

Get the fishmonger to gut, clean and remove the heads of the mackerel. Take a sharp knife and cut the fish down the middle and lay it flat out on the table. Remove any bits of blood or liver that remain and dry and clean with kitchen paper.

Pre-heat the grill to high and take a flat metal dish or grill pan and put two fish side by side. Pour on lemon juice, butter and grind on the black pepper. Keep under the grill until thoroughly cooked through, adding more butter and lemon juice if you think it necessary. Remove from grill, sprinkle over the chopped parsley and keep hot until ready to serve.

Fried Herrings with Mustard Sauce

Another very simple recipe allowing for the freshness of the fish but with a sauce to accompany it which will add a little something extra.

Ingredients

a) Mustard Sauce

1 oz butter
¾ oz flour
½ pt milk
Salt and pepper
1 tsp French or English mustard

b) Rest of the dish

1 herring per person (or two if very small)
4 or 5 tbs medium oatmeal
Salt and freshly ground pepper
1 lemon (cut into four wedges)
Sprigs of parsley for the garnish
Fat or oil for frying.

Method

Get the fishmonger to gut, clean, remove the heads and scrape the scales. Wipe the fish with some wetted kitchen paper, season with salt and pepper and then roll in oatmeal.

Put fat or oil (or a mixture of both) into the pan and when smoking hot, put in the herrings and brown on both sides. This will take about four minutes on each side. Remove from the pan, put on to kitchen paper and pat to remove any surplus fat or oil, put in an ovenproof dish in the oven while you make the sauce.

Mustard Sauce

Melt the butter and stir in the flour. Cook for three or four minutes, diluting with the milk, while slowly bringing to the boil to thicken. Season with salt and pepper, stir thoroughly then add the mustard, stir again and serve.

Finnan Haddock

Ingredients

2 whole smoked fish
1 pt milk
4 fresh eggs
1 bay leaf
4 oz butter
1 tbs fresh chopped parsley
Ground black pepper
½ pt white sauce (using the milk the fish has
   been cooked in)
4 tbs double cream

Method

Cut the fish into four portions using scissors. Put into an ovenproof dish. Cover with milk then add the bayleaf and the butter (cut into dice and spread around). Grind on the black pepper.

Cover the dish with foil and put into a moderate (150°C) oven for twenty-five minutes, (be sure the oven is not too hot or the milk will boil). When cooked remove the bones and then transfer the fish to a serving dish and keep warm.

Make the white sauce using the milk in which the fish has been cooked, finally adding the cream and the chopped parsley. Keep this warm while you poach the four eggs. These should be firm but not hard. Tidy up the egg white by using a pastry cutter and put an egg on the centre of each piece of fish. Quickly heat up the sauce, pour it over the fish and serve.

Cullen Skink

Ingredients

1 lb smoked haddock
2 medium sized onions finely chopped
3 large potatoes, peeled and sliced
10 fld oz milk
2 pinches white pepper
1 pinch salt
2 oz butter

Method

Cook the haddock in a saucepan with the water on a low heat for about fifteen minutes then remove it and put in on a dish and strain the liquid in which it has been cooked into a bowl.

Clean the saucepan and add onions, potatoes and pepper and the liquid from the bowl. Cover the pan and cook until the potatoes are soft.

Remove the skin and bones from the haddock and flake the fish. Next remove the potatoes from their pan and mash them up with the onions and cooking liquid, gradually add the milk, stirring until they are well blended. Return the pan to a low heat and add the flaked fish and butter and stir until the mixture is hot.

Grilled Halibut with Hollandaise Sauce

Ingredients

4 pieces of halibut (at least one inch thick)
Olive oil
Salt and ground black pepper

Method

Wash the fish under the cold tap and dry thoroughly with kitchen paper. Season with salt and pepper and then dip into olive oil.

Put the pieces of fish alongside each other on a grill pan and cook under a moderate heat, turning over each piece until both sides are really well cooked. (Don't forget it is quite thick and will want cooking right through.)

Keep warm in the oven until needed and then garnish each serving with a quarter of lemon and a sprig of parsley.

Hollandaise Sauce

3 egg yolks
4 oz butter

Salt and white pepper
1 tbs lemon juice

Method

The secret of a good Hollandaise is not to let it cook too quickly.

Put a glass bowl over the lower part of a double boiler in which there is very hot – but not boiling – water. Divide the butter into three pieces.

Put one piece in the bowl and when it has melted add the beaten egg yolks and the lemon juice, stirring constantly. Then add the next piece of butter. Continue stirring until it melts, then add the remaining piece.

Remove the bowl from the pan and add the seasoning. If the sauce is too thick, add a few teaspoons of hot water. Serve the sauce separately.

Smoked Mackerel or Trout Pate

Ingredients

1 large fish
Juice of 1 lemon
¼ pint cream
4 oz butter
Pepper and (a little) salt.

Mash up the fish and seasonings and blend them with the (melted) butter. Add cream gradually. Decorate with chives or parsley, and serve with hot toast or French bread warmed.

This recipe can be made with left-overs or

off-cuts of smoked salmon, but the fish will then have to be liquidised rather than mashed by hand.

Haggis

Ingredients

1 sheep's paunch and pluck
1 lb oatmeal
1 lb shredded beef suet
2 medium sized onions
1 tsp pepper
2 tbs salt
½ nutmeg grated
Juice of a lemon
1 ½ pts good stock or gravy

Method

Soak the paunch in salt and water for several hours, then turn it inside out and wash thoroughly several times. Wash the pluck very well, just cover the liver with cold water and boil for 1½ hours. After ¾ hour add the well cleaned heart and lights. Chop half the liver coarsely and chop the other half with the heart and lights very finely. Mix all together and add the oatmeal, finely chopped suet, finely chopped onions, salt, pepper, nutmeg, lemon juice and stock. Press this mixture lightly into the paunch and sew up the opening, allowing space for the oatmeal to swell.

Put the haggis into boiling water and cook gently for 3 hours. During the first hour prick occasionally with a needle to allow steam to escape. Usually no sauce or gravy is served with a haggis but it is a good idea to present it on a bed of mashed potato as it is very slippery and this makes it difficult to dish up. Burns said of the haggis 'It has an honest sonsie (homely) face. Great chieftain o' the pudding race!' A modern haggis is just like its ancestor, a roundish grey-brown sausage.

Some say that haggis is at its best sliced and fried, and served with a puree of 'neeps' – turnips, or more correctly swedes.

Index of Persons

The Scottish clans are so tightly interwoven into history that their names appear on virtually every other page. The list is a long one – the elusive MacAlpine, who claimed royal blood and ruled a loose confederation of clans from Dunstaffnage; Clan Chattan, the 'clan of the cats'; the Campbells with the ducal house of Argyll; clans descended from Somerled, Lord of the Isles, such as the MacDonalds and the MacDougalls; MacLachlan and MacQuarries (the latter now leaderless); MacLaines of Lochbuie and MacLeans of Duart, MacGregors and Camerons, and the many Stewarts – of Lorn, and Appin and Ardsheal – who are more or less closely related to the royal Jacobite family. Most of the clans are still extant and much in evidence in the Highlands and Islands where their castles are familiar landmarks.

Where a general reference is made to them in the text, they are not listed in the index, but some of their most famous scions, from the twelfth century and earlier to modern times, have individual entries under the clan name.

Index of Places

MAPS

To COLL + TIREE
3/4 HRS APPROX

TOBERMORY

DERVAIG

CALGARY BAY

LOCH FRISA

ULVA

STAFFA
FINGAL'S CAVE

LOCH NA KEAL

INCH KENNETH

IONA

LOCH SCRIDAIN

FIONNPHORT

BUNESSAN

BAILE MOR

ERRAID

CARSAIG BAY

THE ISLE OF MULL

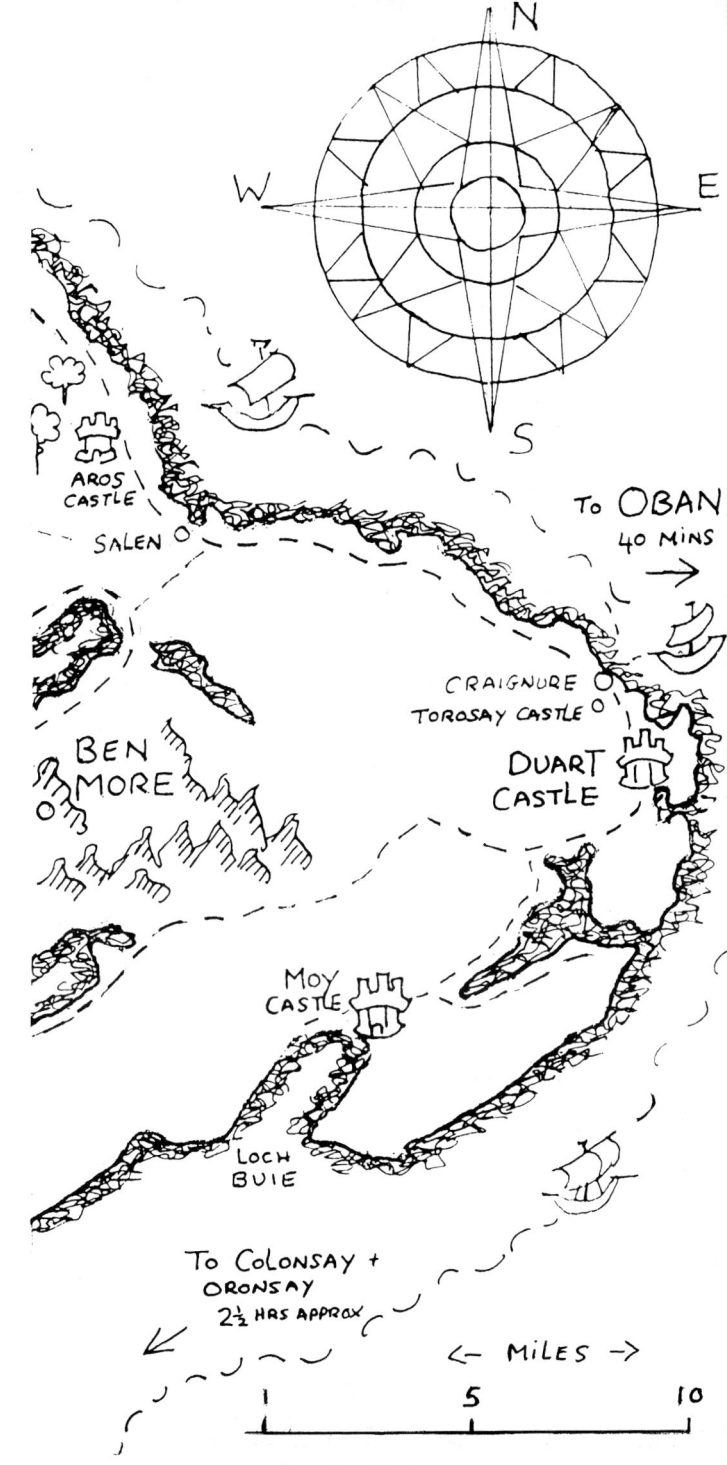

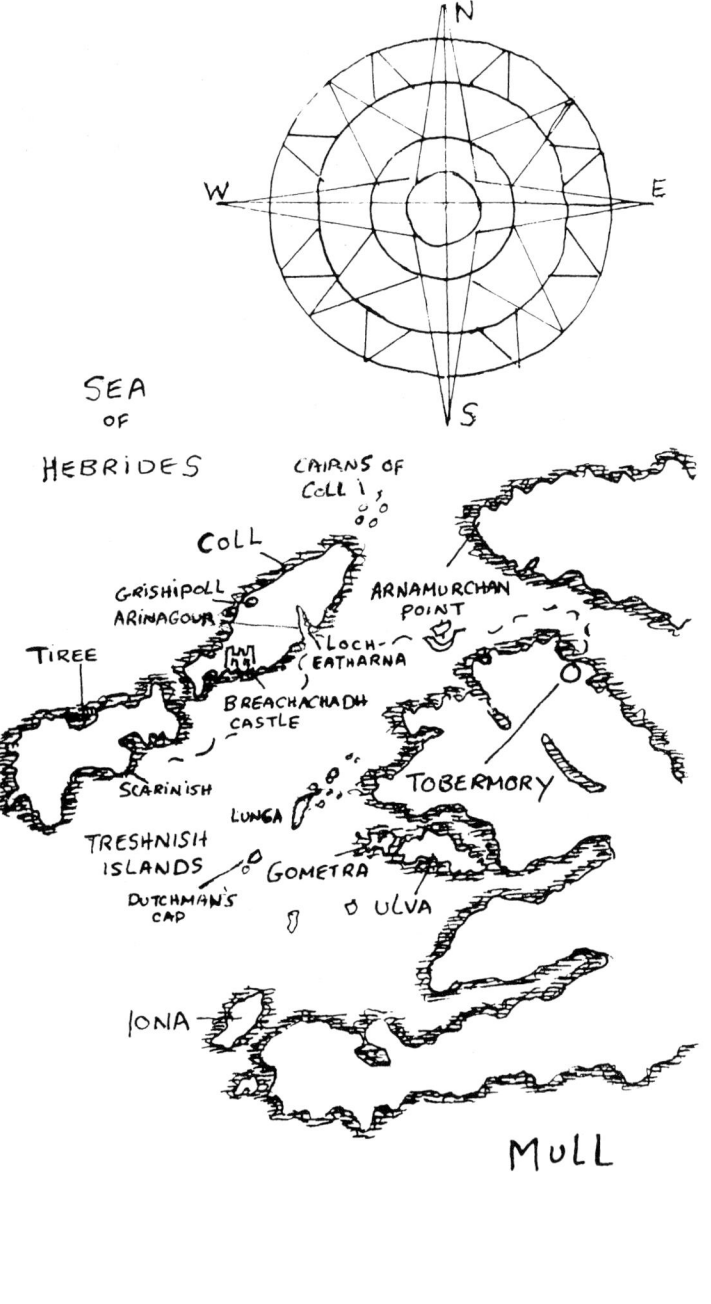

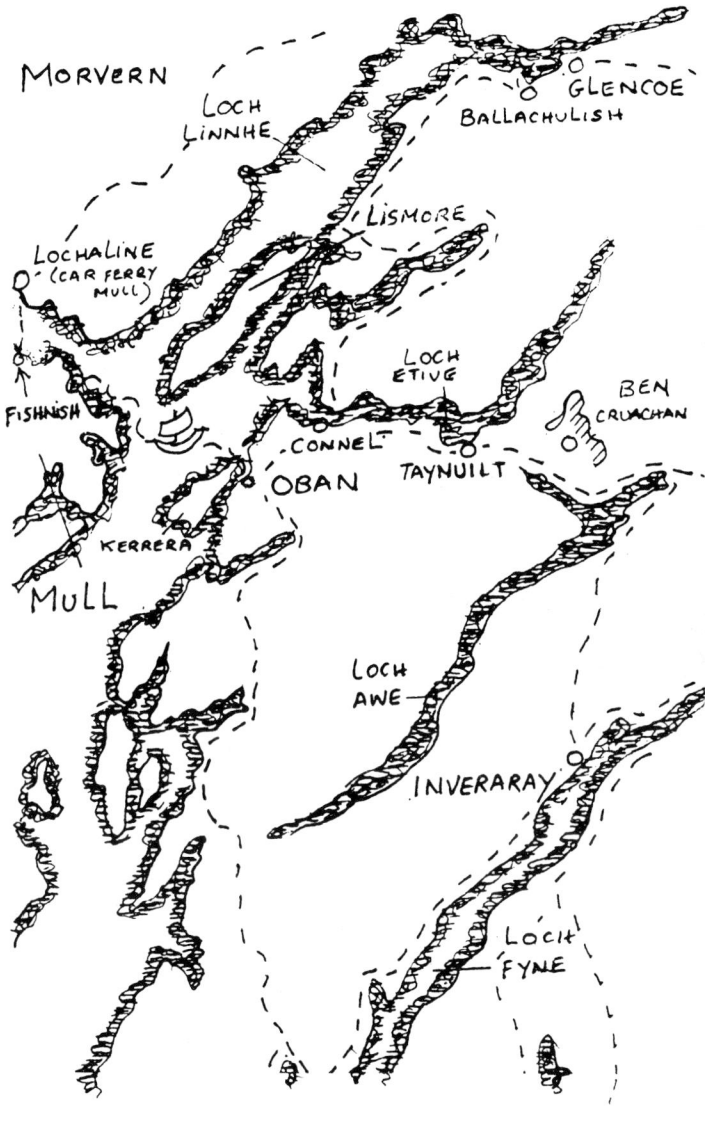

BEN NEVIS
+ FORT WILLIAM

MORVERN

Loch LINNHE

GLENCOE

BALLACHULISH

LISMORE

LOCHALINE
(CAR FERRY
MULL)

FISHNISH

LOCH ETIVE

BEN CRUACHAN

CONNEL

OBAN

TAYNUILT

KERRERA

Mull

LOCH AWE

INVERARAY

LOCH FYNE

MAINLAND SCOTLAND

| 1 | 10 | 20 MILES APPROX |